Forget Wall Street:
Invest in Blue-chip Real Estate

Forget Wall Street:
Invest in Blue-chip Real Estate
A Complete Guide to Housing Investment

Ryan L. Hinricher and Stephen K. Green

Contents

Introduction

What's your IQ? This isn't an intelligence quotient question. It's a question about your Investment Quality. Where are your investments now and what are your goals? This is probably a silly question, as your investment goal is very likely the same as ours, the highest return with the lowest risk, right?

How is our IQ-Investment Quality measured? It's very basic, the quality of your return on investment balanced by risk. We're going to approach rental property investment from a high quality perspective. There aren't any of our IQ measurements published out there, no scoring systems, as we're bringing you an alternative rental property investment approach that isn't part of the mainstream process.

We're not teaching "flipping" or "wholesaling," or "low priced rental property investing." This book is your introduction to "blue-chip" real estate rental property investing. Most investors are familiar with the term "blue-chip" in relation to stock market investments.

A blue-chip stock is one in a large and well-established company with a history of earnings and some product and market advantage. This makes the purchase of their stock shares a higher level investment with the desired result of reasonable and steady returns with lower risk.

A blue-chip real estate investment is a single family rental home with certain characteristics that set it apart from the common rental properties that are the subject of most of the real estate investment publications. These characteristics produce higher returns with lower risk, just like a blue-chip stock investment.

In this book, our goal is to provide the tools and information you need to develop a blue-chip rental real estate investment strategy and implement it successfully. Here's how we're going to do it.

Translate blue-chip to real estate:

We're going to cross over the characteristics of a blue-chip stock market investment to a real estate rental property. You'll learn what those characteristics are, and why they make a certain rental property a "blue-chip" investment.

The thieves of investment return:

While learning what works for blue-chip real estate investment is the primary goal, the best way to ensure success is to know the mistakes that can defeat you in achieving that goal. We're going to tell you about the three thieves of real estate Return On Investment so that you can avoid letting them into your investment plan.

Real estate investment math & leverage:

Learn the calculations and investment formulas for valuation and return on investment. We'll discuss leverage and how to use it properly to increase return without adding significant risk.

Market trends and rare events for profits:

In a thorough discussion of real estate and market trends, you'll see why rental property investment after 2010 has changed dramatically for the better. The events beginning in 2007 forever changed the public's view of real estate and home ownership, and we'll see how investment opportunity was created.

The blue-chip real estate property:

You'll learn the criteria for a rental property to be a blue-chip investment, and how to locate and evaluate blue-chip properties. You'll learn why each selection criteria is important, how to search for properties, and then drill down to the best blue-chip investment selections.

A real-world analysis and property comparison:

Get a thorough knowledge of the process and valuation methods by working through it with real properties. We'll also contrast a blue-chip and a less desirable investment property. You'll learn why buying cheaper homes in some neighborhoods may look like a great investment strategy, but end up being far less attractive in the long term.

Doing the deal – negotiation through closing:

We'll talk about the negotiation process and getting the right property at the right price to achieve your investment goals. Then we'll look at the process involved from the acceptance of the contract through inspections, appraisal, survey and title work to get to a successful closing.

Once you own it – what's next:

Whether you own one property or several, there are certain property management functions and people involved in successfully renting out properties. We'll talk about the professionals and vendors involved and criteria for selection of the best for your needs.

Then the discussion turns to marketing for tenants, tenant interviews, selection and tenant management. There are regulations that must be followed and tenant relations strategies that will contribute to lower vacancy rates and higher profits. We'll look at what is involved in developing a legal and complete tenant application process, forms, and a strong lease.

Structuring your business, growing it & tax strategies:

Because the blue-chip rental property investment strategy is so successful, most investors will grow their business, adding properties and increasing their net worth. We'll look at how to structure the business, and grow it with tax deferral benefits.

The goal of this book is to present to you a complete process and the tools and resources you need to be a successful blue-chip real estate investor. The thorough approach will give you the confidence to use what you learn here and reach your investment goals.

Chapter 1

Blue-chip Investment

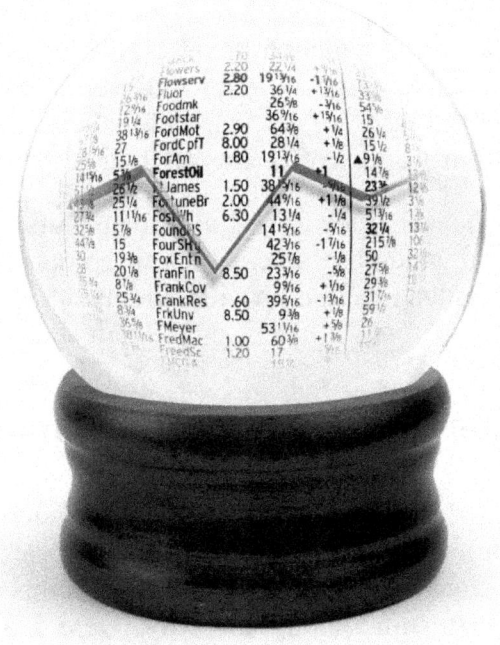

As an investor, you have choices, a great many of them. First you choose the broad investment category, such as stocks, bonds, commodities, etc. Then you move to types of each category, as in dividend paying stocks or growth stocks. And, even after those decision points, you move on to hundreds or thousands of companies or issues from which to choose.

Blue-chip real estate investment can be correlated to blue chip stocks in some ways, and diverges in other very substantial and positive ways. To compare the two, let's develop a thorough understanding of blue-chip stocks and why investors are attracted to them.

Blue-chips & the DJIA

Wikipedia says: *"According to the New York Stock Exchange, a **blue chip** is stock in a corporation with a national reputation for quality, reliability and the ability to operate profitably in good times and bad."*

The most popular index which follows U.S. blue-chip stocks is the Dow Jones Industrial Average. Widely followed since 1928, the DJIA is a price-weighted average of 30 blue-chip stocks chosen because of their quality, reliability and profitability in their respective industries.

Many investors who value lower risk and financially sound companies will only invest in blue-chip stocks. These companies generally are dominant in their industries and provide widely accepted products and services.

Good Press About Blue-chips

In September of 2011, one investment website posted an article titled "5 blue-chips with sweet dividends." Dividends are one aspect of many blue-chip stocks that attract investors hoping for appreciation but wanting some income along the way. Here are the stocks this article recommended:

- **AT&T** – with $125 billion in annual revenue and a 5% dividend, AT&T's entrenched position in the telecommunications industry was also mentioned.
- **Cisco Systems** – a stock that had dropped considerably in value over the previous year, Cisco began paying a 1.5% dividend and some analysts stated that it was undervalued.

- **Walmart** – with revenues and earnings growing every year, even during the economic downturn, and a 2.7% dividend, Walmart is a good buy according to this article.
- **McDonald's** – a 2.7% dividend, 16% rise in revenue and 15% rise in earnings in the quarter ending July 2011 make McDonald's a solid blue chip choice.
- **Pepsico** – with dividend growth of 12.6% over the last 5 years, and a four quarter revenue of more than $6 billion dollars, investors like Pepsico.

These are all very large corporations with names most people readily recognize. They dominate in their industries and markets, even growing in other countries. Investors buy shares in these companies for growth, dividends and a perceived lower risk in tough economic times. However, that's not always the case.

But They're Not Perfect

In April of 2011, The Wall Street Journal posted an article titled "Blues for blue-chip investors." This article came out prior to the July article just mentioned, but is interesting because it talks about investors being "treated badly of late" by blue-chip stocks, and some of the same names just discussed are mentioned.

- **Cisco Systems** – has fallen 38% from recent highs. Of course this was mentioned in the other article as taking the stock to a probable under-valued price, but investors who owned and held it during that period took a beating on price.
- **Walmart** – though only down by 2% in price, the many years of steady growth made some investors nervous when this crack in performance appeared.
- **Others** – Other stocks mentioned as having been unkind to investors included Microsoft down 19% and Johnson & Johnson down 2%.

Over the past decade, the Dow Jones Industrial Average produced an average annual return of 4.7%.

There Is Risk in All Stock Investments

If you go to the Securities and Exchange Commission Investor.gov site, here's how they start the discussion of risk in the stocks, bonds and mutual funds markets:

"When it comes to investing, risk and reward go hand in hand. The phrase "no pain, no gain" – comes close to summing up the relationship between risk and reward. Don't let anyone tell you otherwise: all investments involve some degree of risk. If you plan to buy securities – such as stocks, bonds, or mutual funds – it's important that you understand that you could lose some or all of the money you invest."

Okay, the disclaimer is out of the way, and you'll hear it a lot if you speak to investment advisors or read about market investing. Our two divergent articles bear it out. While all of the stocks mention paid out steady dividends, some took a plunge in price, so investors holding them simply have to sit back and keep holding, waiting for a turn-around in value.

Inflation and The Stock Market

Unfortunately, even buying right, getting a little appreciation in value, and maybe even some dividends doesn't assure us of a profitable long term investment in the stock market. Even blue-chip stocks are subject to inflation risk.

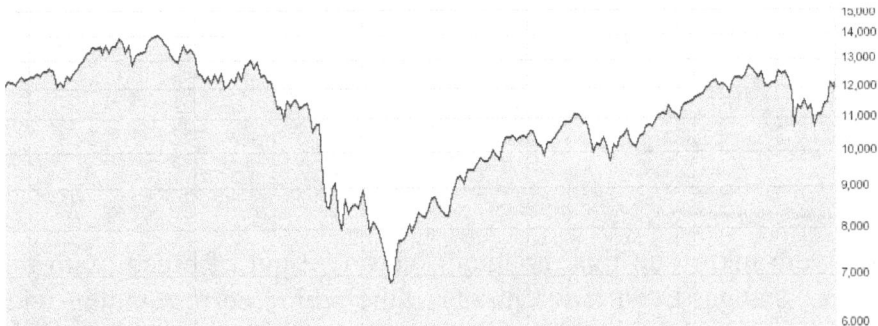

The image above is a 5 year chart of the Dow from January 2007 to January 2011. It's easy to see the price fluctuation and market risk. We're just now back to around where it was in 2008. Even blue-chip stocks are subject to government activities and economic factors that can wipe out price gains, sometimes overnight. Now let's look at the Consumer Price Index for the period from 2001 to 2011, as a chart and a table.

Consumer Price Index - All Urban Consumers

Series Id:	CUUR0000SA0,CUUS0000SA0
Not Seasonally Adjusted	
Area:	U.S. city average
Item:	All items
Base Period:	1982-84=100

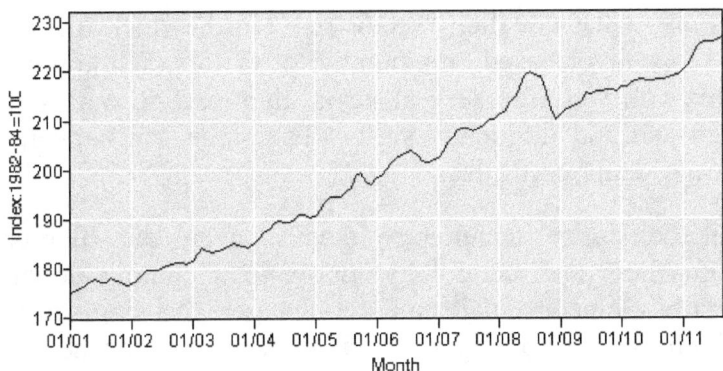

Year	Jan	Feb	Mar	Apr	May	Jun	Jul	Aug	Sep	Oct	Nov	Dec	Annual	HALF1	HALF2
2001	175.1	175.8	176.2	176.9	177.7	178.0	177.5	177.5	178.3	177.7	177.4	176.7	177.1	176.6	177.5
2002	177.1	177.8	178.8	179.8	179.8	179.9	180.1	180.7	181.0	181.3	181.3	180.9	179.9	178.9	180.9
2003	181.7	183.1	184.2	183.8	183.5	183.7	183.9	184.6	185.2	185.0	184.5	184.3	184.0	183.3	184.6
2004	185.2	186.2	187.4	188.0	189.1	189.7	189.4	189.5	189.9	190.9	191.0	190.3	188.9	187.6	190.2
2005	190.7	191.8	193.3	194.6	194.4	194.5	195.4	196.4	198.8	199.2	197.6	196.8	195.3	193.2	197.4
2006	198.3	198.7	199.8	201.5	202.5	202.9	203.5	203.9	202.9	201.8	201.5	201.8	201.6	200.6	202.6
2007	202.416	203.499	205.352	206.686	207.949	208.352	208.299	207.917	208.490	208.936	210.177	210.036	207.342	205.709	208.976
2008	211.080	211.693	213.528	214.823	216.632	218.815	219.964	219.086	218.783	216.573	212.425	210.228	215.303	214.429	216.177
2009	211.143	212.193	212.709	213.240	213.856	215.693	215.351	215.834	215.969	216.177	216.330	215.949	214.537	213.139	215.935
2010	216.687	216.741	217.631	218.009	218.178	217.965	218.011	218.312	218.439	218.711	218.803	219.179	218.056	217.535	218.576
2011	220.223	221.309	223.467	224.906	225.964	225.722	225.922	226.545	226.889					223.598	

If you were hiking up this mountain, you'd be out of breath with the elevation change. Even if we just take the period corresponding with the Dow chart, from 2007 until 2011, there's been around 11.5% inflation. So, those holding stocks from back in 2007 on average are breaking even price-wise, but they've lost 11.5% to inflation. That would have wiped out some or all of the dividends mentioned in the previous articles.

Some stocks do better during inflationary periods if the companies are able to increase prices at the same rate as inflation. However, that isn't always possible, and there is a competitive point when prices just can't go up any more.

Other Risk

There is also what is called "sector risk" in the stock market. Sectors gain and lose favor based on a number of factors. While transportation stocks may do well for several years, they can go out of favor, and equity growth and dividends suffer. The same can happen with any sector, from retail to utilities.

When it comes to technology stocks, even the blue-chips like Microsoft, there are technology innovations coming down the line almost daily. Some are major market-changers, causing some stocks to rise and others to fall precipitously. It's not a sector for the risk-averse.

Increasing Return Outside of Blue-Chips

Those stock market investors who put return at the top of their list for their investments can do far better … or not. Blue-chips are called that because they have reached a point in the business cycle that makes their products or services staples in the American economy. They enjoy stable profits and pay stable dividends. This usually results in slower growth and value appreciation, simply because they're returning some of their profits to shareholders instead of plowing all of it into growth.

On the other side of that coin is the "growth" stock. These can result in stock charts that make a roller coaster look tame. Let's take one big name as an example, Yahoo. Yahoo is a NASDAQ stock, and has never paid a dividend. Investors who bought it in 2002 and held for years did really well, until 2006. Here's the chart:

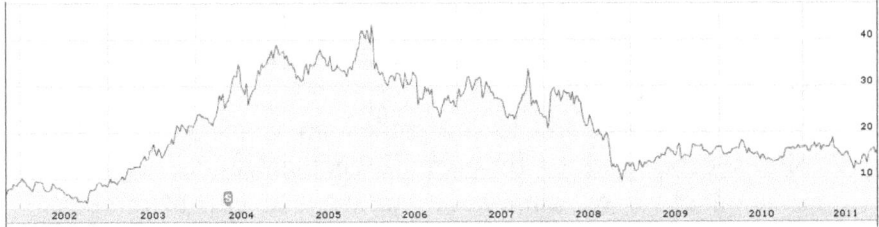

However, if you happened to buy on January 6, 2006 at $43.21/share, on October 20, 2006 your share was only worth $23.21, a drop of 46% in value. It's these dramatic UPS that attract investors, but it's the dramatic downs that can decimate an investment plan. In fact, when this was written, YHOO closed at $15.92/share.

Penny Stocks Could Leave You Penniless

Blue-chip companies don't just appear one day. They are created, then they must be nurtured and grow. If the owners do it right, they could end up on the NYSE or the NASDAQ, get rich, and maybe even make many investors quite happy as well.

However, investors who hope to cash in by getting in on the ground floor of tiny startups through the purchase of "penny stocks" are definitely playing in the most risky sandbox out there. Also called "micro cap stocks," penny stocks are popular because of their price, less than $5/share according to the SEC, but mostly considered as penny stocks by others if they're under $1/share.

There are five main influences that make penny stocks highly risky and make them a poor choice for the serious long term investor:

1. **Lack of company history** – these are normally shares in newly-formed companies, with no performance or earning histories, and some are on the edge of bankruptcy.
2. **Lack of information** – because these companies are not required to file with the SEC, Securities and Exchange Commission, it's very difficult for the investor to get fundamental information about the business, products, services and capitalization.
3. **Liquidity** – these stocks are traded on what is called the "pink sheets," and it's hit-or-miss whether you can buy one in the quantity you want when you want it. This also means that you may not be able to sell either. Dramatic downward percentage price swings happen when a penny stock investor is trying to sell and must keep dropping the price to attract a buyer.
4. **Lack of minimum standards** – there are no minimum standards for company fundamentals or operations to remain listed on the pink sheets, so there's no safety cushion for investors.
5. **Biased recommendations** – one of the reasons it's easy to find penny stock recommendations in articles and all over the Internet is that companies pay people to write them, and also owners of the companies write them. Generating even a small amount of buying interest in a penny stock can

double or triple its value, but once those few buyers are no longer buying, the gains can evaporate just as quickly.

We've taken a tour through the major types of stock investments, from blue-chip down through penny stocks, and the comparative risks and rewards of each. What's the best way to go?

Blue Chips Still The Best Way to Go

Over time, blue-chip stocks are still the way to invest in the stock market for those who want quality, steady returns, appreciation potential, and lower risk.

Our previous charts comparing inflation to the Dow Jones Industrial Average show averages, not specifics. While the average investor may not have raked in the returns after inflation that they would have liked, *average* is the keyword.

The investors who either worked with a good investment advisor or firm, or did their fundamental research and diversified their holdings across sectors, did better than average and bested inflation handily.

The smart blue-chip investor is in it for the long haul, so would have held blue-chip dividend-paying stocks after a drop in value, and they would have benefitted from the recovery. After all, if you don't sell, you haven't experienced a loss. Holding blue-chips for the dividends through the ups-and-downs has historically been an excellent approach to stock market investing.

You don't need to go out and hire a high priced investment advisor to find out what the big players know. Just research what the pension funds and institutions are buying. They either have in-house analysts or hire and follow the best. Their goals are stability, safety, and dividends.

Bonds

You've probably heard the term "flight to safety." Even in the U.S. credit downgrade, investors fled stocks to move to bonds for safety. While bonds do tend to be less risky, they also provide less return as a trade-off for the risk-averse strategy.

Inflation really impacts bonds, as the yield is static over the life of the bond. When inflation flares up, it can eat into bond yields or even wipe out profits completely.

There is a place for bonds and stock shares in every portfolio, but the astute investor is always trying to balance risk and diversify to offset negative results in one market, sector, or investment type. In the next chapter, we'll examine the differences between stocks, bonds, and rental real estate investment. We'll take our "blue-chip" strategy in a different direction.

Chapter 2

Real Estate

Just like blue-chip stocks, there are certain characteristics that make one home stand out among others as an investment opportunity. Some of the same words apply:

- stability
- safety
- cash flow (dividends)
- appreciation

- low risk
- in-demand product
- liquidity

You want all of this in an investment, whether a stock, bond, or a real estate property. Allocation of your investment resources is a major decision. And, we've touched on diversification of a stock portfolio to spread exposure and reduce risk. Diversification of your entire investment portfolio can be improved by allocation of a portion to real estate.

Fundamentals

In blue-chip or any stocks, the fundamentals are about:

- products & services
- inventory costs
- production costs
- operations costs
- pricing advantage
- cash on hand
- debt load
- competitive advantage
- management quality
- assets & asset quality

Institutional investors, pension managers and investment advisors make decisions based primarily on these and other fundamental company factors. They don't invest based on rumor or hype. They don't invest based on chart patterns, you know, all of those formations of price action that are used to predict a stock's price movement based on past movement.

A real estate investment comparison might be buying a rental home based on checking out the recently sold prices of homes in a neighborhood and buying because prices reached a low about three months ago and are starting to rise again. Your decision is based solely on price action, not on fundamentals of the neighborhood (similar to a stock sector), and the home fundamentals. Those include:

- neighborhood quality
- schools
- area employment opportunities
- home characteristics (bedrooms, baths, etc.)
- home features/amenities
- home condition
- area crime statistics
- number of neighborhood homes listed, rented & vacant
- property taxes
- home desirability & functionality

The Penny Stocks of Real Estate

If you've considered rental property investment, you certainly can find a huge amount of information on the Web. There are also many books, courses, seminars and paid consulting arrangements that help investors to buy and sell properties and invest in rental units.

Unfortunately, too many of these programs are constructed around buying cheap houses and maximizing immediate cash flow. While we do want to maximize cash flow as one of the objectives of rental property ownership, it shouldn't be done by investing in properties based mostly on the purchase price.

It's like buying penny stocks, a price-based decision with expectations of growth that very likely will not be in the cards. This price-based decision process leaves out most of the fundamentals that mean the difference between a penny and a blue-chip investment.

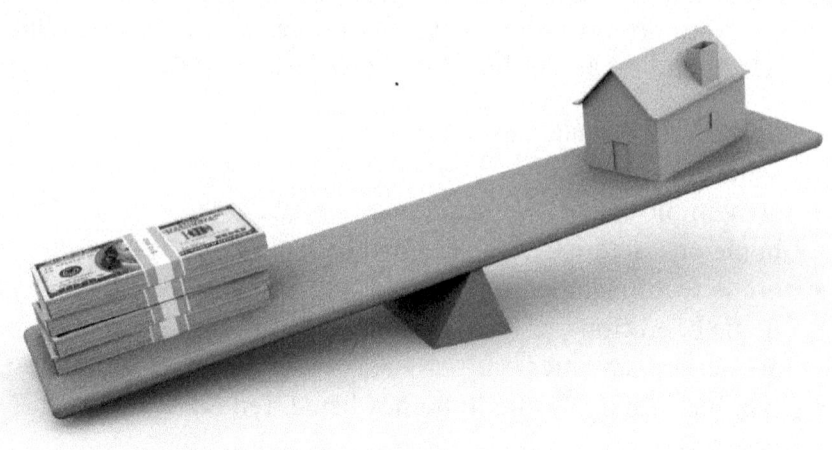

Neighborhood Fundamentals

One common strategy that's taught to many investors is to find out where other investors are buying rental properties and buy there. The theory is that this area is in demand by investors, so it should be a target area for more investment. This could be part of a neighborhood fundamental consideration, but it doesn't take into account other fundamentals, like ultimate liquidity and value appreciation potential.

Too many rental properties in a neighborhood can have a depressing effect on resale prices as well as increase rental competition. This can result in higher vacancy rates or lower rents to keep homes occupied. There are neighborhood fundamentals that should be considered, but basing location decision on what other investors are doing could be a problem.

This is just one example of straying from fundamentals that contribute to a blue-chip rental real estate investment. This book is all about blue-chip real estate, and the fundamentals that must be thoroughly evaluated before an investment.

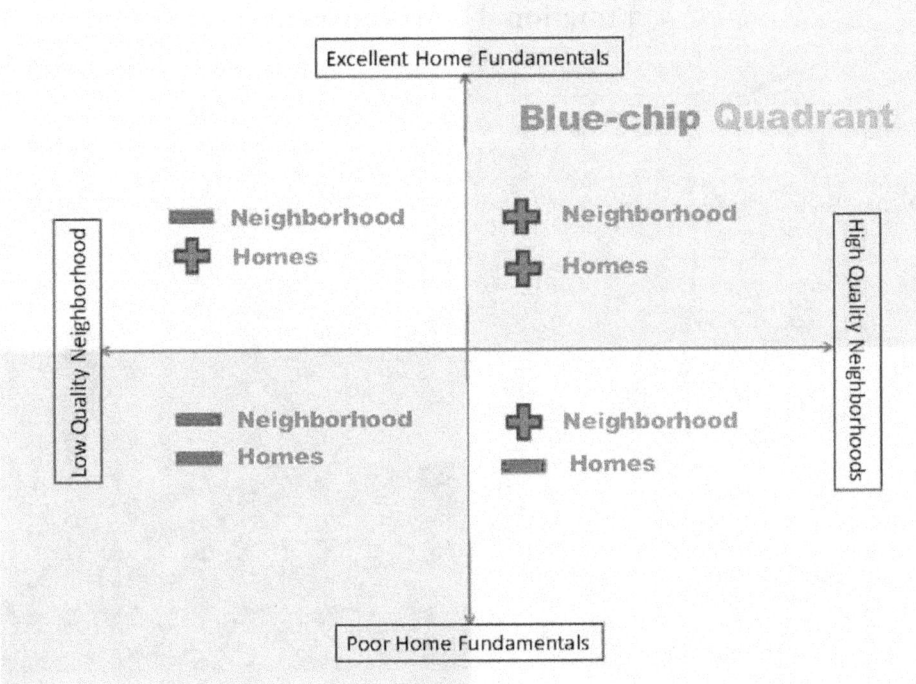

The image gives us a graphic representation of the balance of home fundamentals and neighborhood fundamentals. The rental property investments that we consider blue-chip are those that fall in the upper right quadrant, with excellent neighborhood fundamentals and the same for the home itself.

The "penny" real estate investments fall into the lower quadrants, the worst in the lower left. These would be inexpensive homes in neighborhoods that are stagnant or areas with a lot of foreclosure or rental homes. The price will be attractive, and there will likely also be a few homes in good condition. However, they'll likely be older homes as well, and functional obsolescence is a concern.

Functional Obsolescence

The image above is a great illustration of "functional obsolescence." This kitchen is just plain "out of date." Not only will this home be hard to sell, it will be hard to rent out for optimal rental income. Buyers and renters both want modern amenities and features, from functional floor plans to up-to-date kitchens.

Condition is a Factor

Every buyer, whether for investment or not, wants to purchase a home in good condition and without the need for extensive repair or remodel. It's not that you can't have the work done, or that you can't still realize an acceptable return on investment if the property needs work. However, a blue-chip rental property would more likely be newer and well-maintained by the current owners.

If the furnace needs replacement, it's likely that the air conditioning system will as well. And, if there is a lot of work to do to repair and repaint, it could mean that there are other underlying and structural problems that aren't readily visible.

Ryan Hinricher's Penny Property War Story

Experience is accumulated over time in real estate investing, but sometimes you can get a whole lot of it in a hurry. When I was new in the business I bought some nice properties, some of which I still own today, with steady 7% to 9% returns.

Some people I knew in the business at the time steered me toward some cheaper properties. At a purchase price of $15,000 and needing $10,000 in work, the deal seemed like a good one, as it would rent for around $600/month. A narrow focus on the numbers seemed to provide a great ROI, but in reality I was in for a rough ride.

Quickly it rented on a 12 month lease, the first tenant only stayed for 6 months, leaving without notice. While vacant, squatters broke into the home and took up residence. Corrections required extra security, a fence, and security doors with bars. The home took 3 months to lease.

Things seemed to have improved, as it stayed leased for two years … until the Police Organized Crime Unit called to inform me that my 2 year tenant was a drug dealer and they had raided the home. I managed to get another tenant, but they only stayed for 6 months and left me with $2500 in repairs when I evicted them for non-payment of rent.

It took about 6 months to lease again, but the tenant put up a deposit then skipped out. So, during my ownership, I spent a huge amount of money and lost thousands due to vacancy.

Penny properties require a totally different set of assumptions, including much higher vacancy rates, sometimes 25%-50%, and very high maintenance costs. Meanwhile, my blue-chip properties have a waiting list of tenants, and I've never had a vacancy period of more than two weeks.

Well, we now know what we don't want, even if a lot of investors are flocking to these home purchases. Let's take a look at the basics of a blue-chip rental real estate strategy.

Blue-Chip Rental Property

Why not purchase the BEST product you can?...While you can?

Enter **Blue-chip** Real Estate:

✓ **High-Quality**
✓ **Functional / Newer**
✓ **Pristine Condition**
✓ **Desirable Areas**
✓ **Path of Growth**
✓ **Appreciation Potential**

Why Blue-chip?

If you can buy some cheap houses and rent them out for positive cash flow and maybe get some appreciation when the markets come back, why not? The answer is simply that the blue-chip alternative strategy brings so much more.

1. **Dual Exit Strategy:**
   Investors will discount your property when you sell. Sell to owner occupants. Why buy in neighborhoods dominated by investors?

2. **Better net rental yield:**
   Vacancy, maintenance, and tenant turnover are often grossly understated in non-blue-chip properties.
3. **Less headaches, less hassle:**
   Lower maintenance, lower tenant failure rate, lower tenant turnover.
4. **Lower downside risk:**
   Blue-chip properties are in stable or growing neighborhoods.
5. **Better equity growth potential:**
   Selecting properties in neighborhoods that are in the path of growth, or are considered premium by buyers will result in better appreciation potential.

Part of rental property investment is management, and management can be a hassle. When we emphasize the need to make home condition and age factors important in a blue-chip decision, it's because return on investment shouldn't carry a trade-off in stress. Quality properties reduce maintenance and tenant turnover, both detrimental to our pocketbooks and our life balance.

Holding & Selling Both Work Better With Blue-chips

With a blue-chip rental property, your management and tenant relations tasks will run more smoothly. Your tenants will appreciate a nicer rental than others they considered. They'll enjoy fewer life interruptions and hassles from repair issues. Your tenants will tend to be more stable and willing to pay a higher rent for the nicer property.

As vacancy cost must be factored into investment return, happy tenants make for lower costs. Turnover requires rehab between tenants, a cost that is lower the longer you keep a tenant in the unit. Add in the lost rent between tenants and advertising costs to refill the unit, and it's clear that reducing turnover without cutting rent to do it is a great contributor to return on investment.

When it comes time to sell, the blue-chip property's equity appreciation will outpace the penny stock property significantly. This is especially true when there are a number of these lower priced properties congregated in neighborhoods. They compete against each other and prices drop.

Cash Flow Is Your Dividend

Going back to our blue-chip stock comparison, the cash flow from rental property is the dividend. Rental properties consistently provide cash flows that are multiples of stock dividends. Instead of holding Cisco stock at a 1.5% dividend, or McDonald's at 2.7%, blue-chip real estate investors are happily depositing positive cash flow dollars representing 5% to 20% on their investment. But, there's more.

Tax Advantages Increase Yield

During your ownership of a blue-chip stock, you'll report your dividend earnings each year and pay income tax on them. So, a taxpayer in the 30% bracket getting a 2.7% yield on McDonald's stock is only going to keep 1.9% on their positive cash flow.

A rental property owner who is realizing a 10% positive annual cash flow over mortgage, maintenance, and tax and insurance costs is actually going to pocket more. Consult an accountant about your situation, but the vast majority of rental property real estate investors are able to deduct mortgage interest, taxes, insurance expense, and depreciation against the rental income. As depreciation isn't a cash outlay, it's even better. Instead of pocketing less of the cash received, they're putting more into their bank accounts.

Penny or Blue-chip – A Decision That Really Isn't

So many real estate investors are jumping into the penny property market simply because it's what they're reading about and they're also constantly exposed to the foreclosure news and falling home prices. It seems reasonable to want to buy at the very lowest price as long as there are tenants willing to pay rents that result in good positive cash flow.

It's interesting that an investor who wouldn't think of buying penny or high risk stocks, and only holds blue-chip issues, would quickly jump into real estate rental property purchases that simply don't rise to the level of a blue-chip investment. We believe it's simply because they haven't been educated in the difference, and that's the purpose of this book.

Chapter 3

The Three ROI Thieves

In Chapter 2, we compared penny properties and blue-chip real estate investments. It isn't like there's a line in the sand that you can identify though. It's more flexible to rate them, and we'll think of our property choices as A through D in quality. A is the very best, a true blue-chip, and D is a penny property with a high risk of turning into a horror story.

With this rating scale, we may have considered the property in the Chapter 2 story as a "C," quality investment when it was purchased. It was cheap, but the numbers seemed to indicate a return that was acceptable. In reality it turned out to be a "D-." The best defense against the problems experienced in that investment is to always target A properties. If you've made a minor error, or if the local situation changes a bit, you still have a viable investment, even if it slides into the B range. Maybe a major employer cuts back and lays off employees. This can put some pressure on rents, but you're holding A properties, so you can compete better for the best tenants.

When we get into the next chapter and the math of real estate investment, we'll find a number of calculations to help us to evaluate and place a value on real estate as an investment. Most of these calculations will involve hard numbers that can be easily measured or discovered with research and market analysis.

Taxes, insurance, management and other costs are relatively easy to quantify, budget for, and use to set rents for profits. However, there are three costs that can be elusive but extremely important. These are the three Return on Investment Thieves.

Vacancy & Credit Loss – Thief #1

It is a simple fact; if your income and profits come from collecting rents from tenants, then when there isn't a tenant in the property paying rent, things can get ugly in a hurry.

Notice that there are two parts to that statement:

- there is a tenant occupying the property
- they are paying their rent

Hopefully those two considerations always go together, but reality can be very different. It's a two-part issue, and the real estate investor must get a handle on this reality or suffer the consequences. Vacancy means no tenant and no rent. Credit loss means you have a tenant, but still no rent. And you may have increased costs to do an eviction.

In apartment and large multi-family project investing, vacancy and credit loss are actually less of a problem, as the impact of any given unit being vacant is balanced by the many that are occupied. An apartment investor can look at the past history of the project, determine that vacancy and credit loss has been running 5%, and use that number to budget for the future.

When you're a single family rental property investor, you can't spread the risk over the other units. Sure, if you have multiple rental properties it becomes somewhat less of a risk, however you really experience a 100% loss of income on a single family property when it's vacant or the tenant isn't paying their rent.

In "running the numbers," we can carefully quantify most costs, but this one can be a profit thief that jumps out when least expected and draws down return on investment far more than anticipated.

Example Investment Situation

Let's keep this simple as a cash purchase to allow us to focus on the influence of vacancy and credit loss. You purchase a really cheap home for $45,000, and only have to put $5000 into it to get it ready for rental. This home will rent for $700/month, and you've determined that costs, taxes, insurance, maintenance, etc. will be $300/month.

With $400/month as positive cash flow, and disregarding income tax issues or deductions, this appears to be a great investment, as your return is $400 x 12 = $4800, or 9.6%. You passed on a couple of other opportunities for higher priced homes that would have yielded around 7.5% to do this deal.

Part of that $300/month in expenses was an estimate of 5% in vacancy and credit loss. You came up with that number by doing some local market research and talking to other investors at the local investment club. What you can't really tell from this type of information is whether some of it comes from owners who are charging below-market rents to keep tenants in their units, or if they're just having a good year.

That 5% you allowed amounts to only $420/year, just over half a month's rent. So, you've predicted that your unit will only be vacant for a couple of weeks between tenants. And, you're expecting that to happen only once a year by using 12 month leases. Being careful, $300/year was also budgeted into your costs for rehab between tenants, repainting, etc. That was part of the $300/month in costs.

You get your first tenant in right away, and things are rocking along smoothly for about six months. The tenant is late on rent, and you haven't seen them for a few days. After a week, you're knocking on the door to see what's going on. In looking in the window, you see that the place is empty. You go in and find that they've left you with some damage, and they're definitely gone.

So, you have the normal budgeted $300 for rehab, and we'll ignore the fact that they left you with some extra repairs. Right now we're just dealing with vacancy and credit loss. You are out one week's rent already, and it's going to take you at least three more weeks to get the repair work completed. You advertise the unit as available, but it takes another month to rent it. Let's look at our return now.

- seven weeks rent lost, approximately $1140
- Original $4800 profit less $1140 = $3660
- $3660 divided by $50,000 invested = 7.3% return
- that's 24% less than you anticipated going in

You're now down to the yield you passed up on your other choices. If your vacancy period had stretched by another two weeks, or if they had been another two weeks behind in rent, your ROI would have dropped to 6.6%, a whopping 31% hit.

The simple fact is that C and D quality properties usually carry a higher rate of credit loss and stay vacant longer than blue-chip A and B quality properties. This example is actually quite normal, not a horror story at all. When you're investing in penny properties, you can't ignore the higher risk of vacancy and credit loss. Once you face up to the reality, if you add these risks into the property evaluation, you'll find that paying more for the blue-chip is a wiser decision in almost every case.

Maintenance & Repairs – Thief #2

We kept extra repair costs out of our previous example, but they're very much a concern for rental property investors. When evaluating investment property choices, extensive research of the neighborhood and the ages of the homes is a must. Older homes require more maintenance and repairs are more costly.

In 2007, the National Association of Home Builders published a report titled "Study of Life Expectancy of Home Components." Here are some of the replacement ages for home components:

- Appliances
    o   gas range – 15 years
    o   dryers & refrigerators – 13 years
    o   compactors – 6 years
    o   dishwashers – 9 years
    o   microwave ovens – 9 years
- Electrical accessories & lighting controls – 10 years
- Kitchen & bathroom faucets – 15 years
- Security systems & smoke detectors – 5 to 10 years
- Heating, ventilation & air conditioning systems
    o   furnaces – 15 to 20 years
    o   heat pumps – 16 years
    o   air conditioning – 10 to 15 years
    o   electric or gas water heater – 10 years

As far as repair and replacement costs for these home components, even the simplest of repair visits are in the $200 to $300 range, and replacement of appliances in the $1000 to $2000 range. As far as HVAC, Heating, Ventilation & Air Conditioning, an entire system can run between $5000 and $15,000 depending on area and efficiency.

Obviously, age of the home is a major consideration with the costs of these type of repairs and component replacement. And, age enters into the price at which you can buy. So, C and D rated homes will normally be older, and the investor must factor in these anticipated repairs and replacements. In doing so, you can quickly find the annual ROI evaporating.

Taking our previous example, if you didn't budget for replacement of a furnace, and it becomes necessary at a cost of $1500, your return drops from 9.6% to 6.6%, again a 31% hit. Just hope that you don't have the vacancy problem that same year!

Tenants in C and D neighborhoods and homes can also tend to be less careful about their treatment of the home and the fixtures and appliances. If the surrounding homes are in disrepair, there is little incentive for your tenants to exhibit concern for your property. Repairs will become more frequent and costs will rise.

One striking example is with air conditioning. Other than full replacement, the highest cost of repair is the replacement of the compressor. The failure of the tenant to change the air filter regularly frequently damages or completely destroys the compressor valves, resulting in expensive repairs of $1000 to $2500.

An A or B rated blue-chip property doesn't necessarily have to be newer. If the previous owners have replaced major components, and those are relatively new, and they've taken good care of the structure, the home can be a blue-chip even though it's not a spring chicken.

Tenant Turnover – Thief #3

If you're in the restaurant business, table turnover is a good thing. The more meals you can serve with a certain number of tables, the higher your profits. However, turnover isn't a good thing in rental property investing.

Parts of the tenant turnover calculation are not too difficult to quantify. You know that when a tenant moves out you must:

- do minor patching and painting, and you know what that costs on average
- lose rent for a period of time, but you know that it's usually less than two weeks or some number you have learned from experience
- advertise the property, and you've budgeted for that

There could be unexpected repairs, but hopefully some or all of that expense is covered by a repair deposit.

Blue-chip to Penny Investment Comparison

One of the characteristics of a blue-chip property is the ability to retain tenants for longer lease periods. These are nicer properties in better neighborhoods with schools that are in-demand. There is far less of a tendency for renters to move and make their children change schools. Also, blue-chip homes are nicer, better maintained, and the tenant doesn't want to "trade down." Let's do a five year comparison to see the influence of turnover on return.

The Penny Property

We're purchasing a low priced home with the goal of one year leases. We paid $35,000 (cash again for simplicity in comparison) for this home, repairs included, and we can rent it out for $750/month with $300/month in expenses.

Our expense estimate is based on reasonable reality of 12 month leases going to term, $300 in rehab between tenants, and no other or unexpected repairs. So, we're expecting $300 in rehab per year as part of our costs of $300/month, as our 12 month tenant moves out and a new one is installed. Our expectation is to lose two weeks rent each year to rehab and re-lease the unit. Our gross positive cash flow is $450/month taking into account the rehab, but not the lost rent, so our gross cash flow is for 11.5 months, or $5175/year. That's a nice anticipated return of 14.7% barring any early move-outs or bad credit problems, so means that everything is exactly going per our plan.

However, even the best-laid plans can go the wrong way. Remember the horror story in the last chapter. Let's see how a similar situation, with numbers much like this example penny property deteriorated rapidly in a five year (60 month) holding period.

- Though our plan was for 12 month leases, it turns out that we could only get one tenant to stay a full 12 months.
- Seven tenants stayed for full 6 month leases, but moved on at the end of the lease. Extra cost: $300 rehab extra time each year for those 3 years (42 months) = $1050.
- Lost rent extra cost of two weeks x 3 extra move-outs = $1125.
- One tenant damaged the property extensively expecting eviction, which took one month with no rent and they were another month behind.
  - Lost 2 month's rent for non-payment = $1500.
  - Damage over security deposit cost $600.
  - Lost another month's rent to make repairs and re-lease = $750.
- Number of rental homes in neighborhood jumped, conditions deteriorated, rent had to be reduced to keep tenants. Rent was reduced last 3 years (36 months) to $650/month = $3600 lost income.
- Let's add up the numbers from the items above:
- $1050 + $1125 + $1500 + $600 + $750 +$3600 = $8625

- Anticipated GOI for 60 months was $5175 x 5 = $25,875
- Actual GOI was $8625 less = $17,250
- $17,250 / 5 years = $3450/year = 9.8%

This isn't a fairy tale. Unfortunately, there are a great many stories just like it in the low-priced rental home market. Had the investor not reduced the rent, the damage would have just transferred from reduced rent to long vacancy periods. It could have been worse. This investor's return was 33% less than the plan going in.

However, in this neighborhood, due in part to the prevalence of rental homes, values appreciated less than 2% for the entire period. The value of the home didn't even keep pace with inflation.

The Blue-chip Property

We locate a blue-chip opportunity, and we pay $85,000 for a home that we can rent out for $1100/month. In this neighborhood, 12 month leases are the norm, and we are going to get a bonus that's common, as one tenant is going to stay through two lease periods. The schools are excellent and tenants want to be stable for their children's education. Actually, most of our blue-chip rentals are experiencing more like 3 tenants per 5 year period. We'll just be conservative here. We're looking again at a 5 year period.

Our Projection: Our costs, including an estimated $300 rehab between tenants is projected to be $400/month. Using these numbers, our projected return is $1100 - $400 = $700 x 11.5 months = $8050 for each year based on 12 month leases.

This is 9.4% based on our purchase price, which is slightly less than our penny property's actual return above. However, our newer home in an in-demand neighborhood has a waiting list of tenants, so our lost rent between tenants shrinks by half to one week. And, we're going to keep one tenant for two years.

Here's how the numbers shake out:

- reduction of $300 rehab for one tenant staying through two lease periods.
- Instead of 2 weeks between tenants, we're experiencing only 1 because we have a waiting list. Extra income over 5 year period for three tenants who stayed 12 months each = $256 x 3 =$768.
- full extra month of income (over projection) due to the two year occupancy without lost rent between tenants = $1100.
- Rents were raised year 3 by $50/month, year 4 by $75/month, year 5 by 50/month for extra income over the 5 years of $2100.
- $300 + $768 + $1100 + $2100 = $4268 in extra income
- $8050 x 5 + $4268 = $44,518
- That's $8904/year, or a 10.4% real return.

However, this home is in an in-demand neighborhood, and this area experienced a 6% appreciation over the 5 year period. This home is now worth $90,000+.

Both of these homes were calculated with pretty normal rental situations. The blue-chip property always holds tenants longer, reducing turnover and costs between tenants. There is far more risk of unpleasant and unbudgeted situations with penny properties...don't forget that story in the previous chapter.

In fact, we've experienced 3 to 5 year same-tenant rental stays in some of our blue-chip rental homes, with happy tenants not wanting to take on the hassle of moving. And, our properties compare very well with the nicer rentals they see at the same or higher rents. That ROI number jumps significantly if you only have two tenants in that five year period.

The Three Thieves Make a Major Difference

Taking all of these factors into account, vacancy and credit risk, repair and maintenance, and turnover risk, there is ample evidence that blue-chip real estate investing will consistently produce higher returns with less risk than the cheaper rental properties.

Chapter 4

The Math of Real Estate Investment

The most profitable and successful real estate investors hold one concept in high regard: "you embrace the numbers, not the house." Sure, they scrutinize a potential rental home as to location, amenities, features, condition and appeal, but those aren't the things that get them excited and bring them to the closing table. It's the *numbers.*

You make money in four basic ways with real estate:

1. Cash Flow
2. Appreciation
3. Loan Amortization (if you're getting a loan)
4. Tax Shelter

Every property is unique, and the contribution each of these factors make to your return on investment will vary. One property may yield excellent cash flow, while another will not provide as much cash, but will bring a great return when it's sold due to your bargain purchase price. Another may be ideal for tax reasons related to your investment portfolio.

In this chapter we're going to run through a number of financial and valuation calculations used by real estate investors. Some you may find useful, and others you may never need. However, it never hurts to know what they are and their use, as you may have a seller throwing them around in a negotiation.

Also, there will be calculations explained that are used mostly by commercial and multi-family real estate investors. They may only have marginal value in the evaluation of a single family home for purchase.

However, many successful single family investors move on to multiple units, apartments, and even office complexes as they grow their portfolios. We'll give you what you need to know if you do, and you can just pull this book down off the shelf and jump right in when opportunity presents itself.

Calculations Require Data – Garbage In...

We've all heard the saying "garbage in – garbage out," usually used in business and computer programming to make clear that the results of any information resource, calculation, or computer program can be very dramatically altered based on the data that goes in the front end.

In real estate investing it's no different. You can't make reliable investment decisions or come up with accurate valuation calculations if your underlying data isn't accurate and carefully gathered. Purchasing real estate requires that you do the "due diligence" necessary to feed reliable data into your process. It's the only way that you'll get a reliable investment result.

The first few items that follow will apply to any property, and will be on your checklist for a single family rental home. The others apply more to multi-family properties, but we'll be looking at calculations that will need this type of data, so we'll quickly run through them here.

Property Information

This applies even in purchasing a new home for the family. You of course will want to know the characteristics of the property that make it suitable for your needs, and those of the tenants you'll be renting to.

Condition is critical. We're blue-chip investing, and we've already discussed the age of a property, and how age and condition can change your income results substantially.

"Location, location, location..." It will never change for real estate. Rental property value is very dependent upon neighborhood characteristics, the local economy, and nearby schools.

Utility Costs

Utilities for most single family rental properties are paid by the tenant, but not always. It's best to know what they are whether you or the tenant will be paying, as they may ask. If they're hitting the upper end of their rent payment ability, you don't want to have them leave prematurely because they find that they can't afford to heat and cool the home.

Market Rents

Whether a property has been in rental service or not, you need to know what you can charge for rent in order to evaluate the investment for cash flow and return. This involves comparing similar properties in the nearby area that are renting.

You can ask your property manager,call as a prospective tenant on rental ads, ask a few questions about the property characteristics and what the rent will beIf you're working with an investment property company, call a 3rd party property manager to validate what they say it will rent for. Try to get as many comparable property rents as you can, then drive by them to get a feel for how they compare to the one you're evaluating for purchase. You may be able to charge more or may have to charge less.

You Want a Cash Flow More Than a P&L

If you're buying a property that's already been in rental service, particularly a multi-family or office property, you'll want to see their Profit and Loss, but even more you'll want to see a cash flow analysis. Why? There may be items in the P&L that are more perks for the owners than necessary expenses for the business.

If that's the case, those items can be backed out of the expenses to reflect a better performance. You'll only back them out if you're going to do away with them when you take ownership.

Do a very thorough analysis of income and expenses if the property has been in rental service. When you're looking at expenses, see if there are ways in which you can cut them once you take ownership. As for rental income, let's look at the next item.

Are the Leases and Income Real?

If a property is rented, examine all leases carefully, note when they expire and compare them to current market rents. Some landlords will charge below market rents to entice tenants to stay longer because they don't like finding and interviewing new tenants.

Ask for actual bank records, statements from the property management company,or cancelled checks to compare to the amounts in the leases. There are cases where landlords cut verbal deals with tenants to pay less in exchange for services, or just because they're having a hard time and they don't want to force them out.

Now you have a feel for the type of data you'll be feeding into the calculations we're about to explore. To begin, the one that you'll definitely want to get right is the CMA, Comparative Market Analysis. This isn't technically a formula or straight calculation, but it is one that you or a trusted real estate professional should do for every home you're considering buying.

CMA, Comparative Market Analysis

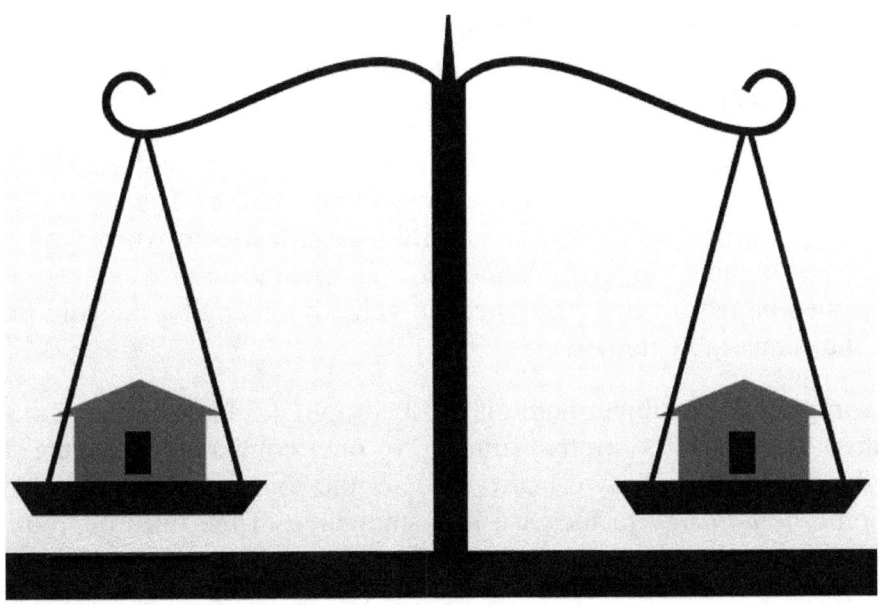

This is an exercise to illustrate how real estate professionals come up with the price they advise their sellers to make the listing price of the home. It's also how buyer agents determine for their buyers if a home they're considering for purchase is priced properly in the market.

Locate Comparable Sold Properties

You first step is to find properties that have sold recently and are as similar as possible to the one you're evaluating (the subject property). These are your major considerations:

- The sold properties be as nearby as possible, same neighborhood preferably.
- They have sold as recently as possible, preferably in the last couple of months.
- They be as similar as possible to your subject property in features, bedrooms, baths, lot size, square footage, garage type and size, and amenities.

If sold prices are not public record in your area, you'll need to get a friendly real estate professional to pull them for you from the MLS, Multiple Listing Service.

You need a bare minimum of three comparables to do a decent job, so you may have to vary a bit in the comparable features. If so, get a local appraiser's figures or go to a website like Zillow.com where you can get approximate values of home renovations and improvements. You can then adjust for the differences in value by changing the sold price of the comparable homes.

Example: Your subject home is a 3 bedroom 1.5 bath property. In all other respects it's pretty similar to one comparable, except the comparable has only two bedrooms. So, the sold price of that "comp" should be ***adjusted*** to increase it by the value of the third bedroom it didn't have.

If you have a local appraiser willing to give you some numbers for the value of bedrooms, baths, family rooms, decks, etc., that would be the best way to go. We're not looking for nailing it on the head, just reasonable estimates. In checking out websites for the "value of adding bedroom," we found several that placed the value between 5% and 7% of the home's value, depending on whether you are going from a 2 to a 3 or a 3 to a 4, etcetera.

Going from a 2 to a 3 bedroom home carried the highest premium, so we'll use 7% for this example.

- Comparable home sold for $82,000 with 2 bedrooms.
- We add 7%, $82,000 x 1.07 = $87,740, our new sold price

You do this for differences in bedrooms, baths and other important feature differences, and it's the way appraisers do it as well. So, once you've adjusted your comparable homes' sold prices, you can do your CMA calculation.

- Home A adjusted sold price of $87,740 (1520 sq ft)
- Home B sold price of $88,900 (1600 sq ft)
- Home C adjusted sold price of $86,200 (1500 sq ft)
- Home D sold price of $89,500 (1630 sq ft)

Then you take each sold price and divide by the square footage to get price per square foot.

- Home A - $87,740 / 1520 = $57.72/square foot
- Home B - $88,900 / 1600 = $55.56/square foot
- Home C - $86,200 / 1500 = $57.47/square foot
- Home D - $89,500 / 1630 = $54.91/square foot
- Then we average those to get $56.42 average/sq ft

Our subject home is 1580 square feet in size. So, we multiply that average sold price per square foot times 1580 to come up with an approximate market value of our subject home of $89,144.

So, if it's listed at less than that, we're on the right track to try and negotiate it down even more to get a bargain. However, there's one more thing you need to do ... another CMA! What? Well, by nature, a past sold price is past history. No matter how recent, it's not necessarily indicative of the current market. So, just do the exact same process again, but do it with comparable properties listed for sale right now. This will give you a clear picture of where the subject property is situated price-wise in the market. Knowing this gives you a starting point for negotiations.

Don't get freaked out about a CMA, as it's all about estimates. It's a starting point to determine what you think you'll have to pay for the property. Then you can apply some other calculations, including market rents for comparable properties, to determine if it's a good investment. To simplify the process, you can call an appraiser familiar with the neighborhood and ask him or her to "comp out" the property. They may charge you a few bucks but they will save you the time.

Gross Scheduled Income

Gross Scheduled Income (GSI) is the income that's expected from the property if all rents are collected when due and as estimated. So, if your plan is to rent out a home for $850/month:

$850 x 12 = $10,200 – Gross Scheduled Income

Gross Operating Income

Remember our discussion of vacancy and credit loss and their impact on your return. Gross Operating Income (GOI) is the Gross Scheduled Income from above less your actual or estimated deduction for vacancy and credit loss:

$10,200 GSI - $1500 V & CL = $8,700 Gross Operating Income

Operating Expenses

This isn't a calculation per se, it's more of a clarification of how you come up with operating expenses; what's included and what's not.

Expenses that are necessary to operate the property are operating expenses. This DOES NOT include mortgage payments, interest, and capital expenditures. You wouldn't include improvements to the property, as they are capital expenditures. Property taxes are operating expenses, but your personal income tax liability on profits is not an operating expense.

Repairs and maintenance, as well as management costs, landscaping, and advertising are all operating expenses. However, adding a room would not be, as it's a property improvement.

Net Operating Income

Now that we know how to calculate Gross Operating Income (GOI) and our operating expenses, we can determine our Net Operating Income (NOI). It's the difference between the two:

$$GOI - Operating\ Expenses = NOI$$

CFBT & CFAT (Cash Flow Before & After Taxes

Once we have our NOI, Net Operating Income, we can determine two different cash flows for our investment. One is before our personal tax liability and the other is after. They both start with NOI, but they are like two different directions, a fork in the road.

That's because there are income and non-cash deductible expenses involved in real estate investing. While depreciation isn't cash out of pocket, you get to deduct it in most cases. The interest on your mortgage payments is also deductible. Should you have any money in deposits or escrow accounts that's earning interest, that would be income for taxes.

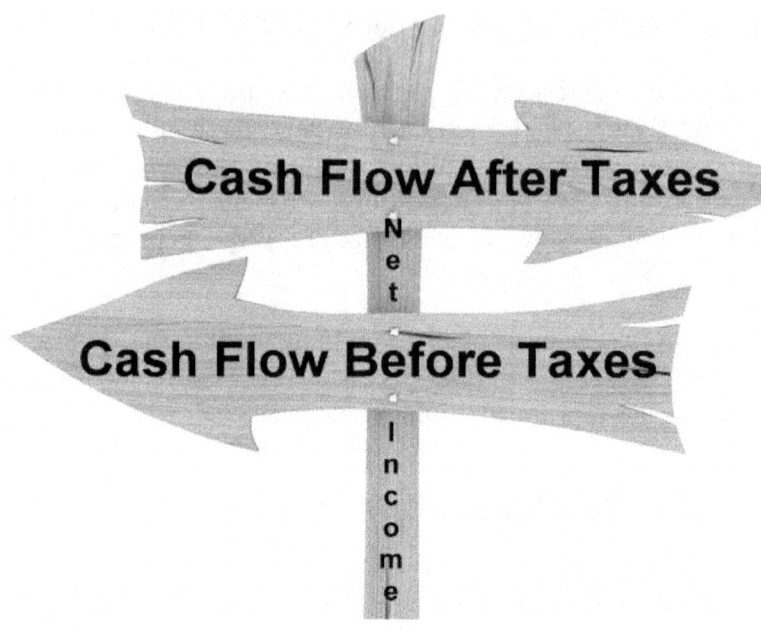

Cash Flow Before Taxes	Cash Flow After Taxes
(-)Debt Service	(-)Interest Paid
(-)Capital Expenditures	(-)Depreciation & Amortization
(+)Interest Earned	(+)Interest Earned

Start with your NOI, Net Operating Income. This is the cash flow after your operating and out-of-pocket expenses. As shown by the minus signs on the left side of the table, you deduct your debt service (mortgage payments) and any capital expenditures, then add in any interest you earned on deposits. This gives you your Cash Flow Before Taxes.

On the right side, we get to deduct our interest paid on the mortgage, and depreciation/amortization. If we earned any interest, we must add it in to pay taxes on it. However, we're deduction interest we paid on the mortgage which was cash out of pocket, but also depreciation which was not.

At the time this was written, you could depreciate a residential rental property over 27.5 years. So, each year, you'd get to deduct 1/27.5 of the cost of the property. Since it didn't come out of your pocket, it decreases your taxable income and puts more money into your pocket as cash flow after taxes.

Capitalization Rate or Cap Rate

The Capitalization, or Cap, Rate of a real estate asset is the relationship of the NOI, Net Operating Income to the current value of the asset. It's a way to evaluate the performance of the asset to compare it to other investments the owner could make with the money tied up.

We've already determined how to calculate NOI in this chapter, so finding the current value of a property, we can then calculate the Capitalization Rate. Here's the formula:

$$\text{Capitalization Rate} = \frac{\text{annual net operating income}}{\text{cost (or value)}}$$

Using that formula, if an investor has a small six unit apartment project currently valued at $500,000, and it's generating an NOI of $50,000/year:

$50,000 / $500,000 = 0.10 or 10% Cap Rate

Cap rate is a good calculation to apply because it's used by so many investors, bankers, and others involved in the real estate market. It's also easy to calculate if you know the NOI and value. This makes it a good way to compare the performance of various properties.

It is important to understand that the Cap Rate calculation isn't influenced by cash flow. As NOI is the GOI, Gross Operating Income, of the property less "operating" expenses, it doesn't include the mortgage. So, an investor can over-mortgage the property, severely damage cash flow, and still show a good Cap Rate number.

However, Cap Rate is a tool based on a snapshot of performance, a look at the property at a certain moment in time. It doesn't look at the performance of a property over time, the entire length of the investment.

Gross Rent Multiplier (GRM)

The GRM, Gross Rent Multiplier, is a very simple calculation of relative value of a property based on the amount of gross scheduled rent income it generates.

GRM = Market Value / Gross Annual Scheduled Income

and transposed:

Market Value = GRM x Gross Annual Scheduled Income

The simplicity of this calculation makes it a great way to quickly compare a long list of potential investment properties to see which deserve more investigation. It's not accurate enough of a valuation tool to do much more than that, but it helps to narrow the field.

Since you're dividing the value (larger number) by the gross scheduled income number which is smaller, this means that the lower the GRM, the better. An example would be a property worth $100,000 that generates gross scheduled rent income of $50,000/year.

$100,000 / $8,400 = 11.9 GRM

If this same property delivered higher rents, making the gross scheduled income $11,000:

$$\$100,000 / \$11,000 = 9.1\ GRM$$

So, the property that generates higher rents for the same value has a lower GRM. When an investor has a list of properties and wants to see which she should concentrate on first, checking out the lower GRM numbers is the way to go.

Cash on Cash Return

Cash on Cash Return is the ratio between an annual cash flow number and the amount of cash invested in the property. Normally, the investor uses the CFBT, Cash Flow Before Taxes, number.

Cash on Cash Return is a popular investment tool because it allows an easy comparison to other types of investments and their yields. It's normally calculated on the first year's cash flow before taxes and the cash the investor put into the deal to buy the property. So, there is a vast difference in the return numbers between a financed property and one purchased with cash ... leverage.

Example cash purchase:

$100,000 property purchased all cash. We'll ignore closing costs to simplify the calculation. Operating expenses are $200/month. The investor has $100,000 invested in the deal. The property rents for $800/month = $9600/year less $2400 expenses, leaving a NOI, Net Operating Income of $7200/year.

$$COC\ Return = NOI / Cash\ Invested$$

$$COC\ Return = \$6000 / \$100,000 = 7.2\%$$

Example financed purchase:

We'll take the same home and expenses, but we'll mortgage the property with 20% down. Now we have $20,000 cash invested, but we also have a mortgage payment. This payment will reduce our cash flow. At 5% mortgage interest, the payment would be $429/month, or $5148/year. We still have our $200/month in expenses, or $2400/year.

$9600 Rents – $2400 Expenses - $5148 Debt Service = $2052

$2052 Cash Flow / $20,000 Cash Invested = 10.2% COC Return

These examples show the value of leverage in real estate investing. This investor is now free to go out and replicate this deal four more times if they want. If it were replicated exactly for example, that would be cash flow of $2052/year x 5 homes = $10,260/year in cash flow, and the same 10.2% return on cash invested.

However, that's just part of the story. Also, this investor has five times the investment value for appreciation. Should the value of real estate increase only 5% over the next five years, the leveraged investor would have $500,000 in properties, resulting in appreciation of $25,000. The cash buyer would only see $5,000 in appreciation.

Then there is the increased annual return from increasing rents. Here's a graph of a very similar situation showing the difference in Cash On Cash appreciation over 10 years instead of an all cash purchase.

In this case we used the property analysis application, RealYields to show the Cash on Cash return for both a financed purchase and a cash purchase over a 10-year horizon.

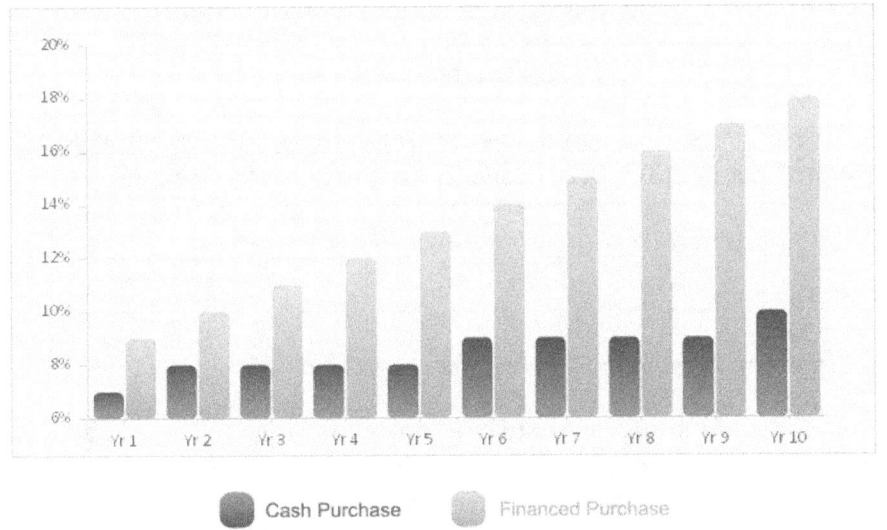

Annual Cash on Cash Return (From Rent)

Cash Purchase   Financed Purchase

(courtesy: realyields.com)

Price-to-Rent Ratio

Before we get into the Price-to-Rent ratio, we can get a head start on understanding it if we think about P/E ratios of stocks on the exchange. The P/E, or Price-to-Earnings ratio of a stock is the price it's currently selling for per share divided by its annual earnings per share.

P/E = Share Price / Annual Earning/Share

so

$35 Share Price / $1.50 per share annual earnings = $23.33 P/E

Investors compare the P/E ratio of stocks in the same industry to locate value. In finding a stock that can be purchased with a lower P/E, they're getting higher earnings for the money invested. It's called a "multiple," because the stock share price is a certain calculated multiple of earnings. P/Es can rise when investors are expecting better future earnings and buy the stock in anticipation of better returns.

Price-to-Rent Ratio

All of the players who had a stake in pumping up the housing market before the bust in 2007 were prone to say the same two things:

"A home is the best investment you'll ever make."

and

"Renters throw money down the drain."

Buying versus renting is really a moving target. It's a changing condition based on complex relationships between home prices, rents, financing costs, inflation, and other factors. And, "real estate is local" is also a saying that holds true. Markets differ significantly.

One real estate search site that publishes a price-to-rent ratio is Trulia.com. They compare the total cost to own a home to the cost to rent. Ownership costs include:

- mortgage principal and interest
- property taxes
- insurance
- closing costs
- HOA (Homeowner Association) dues if there are any
- mortgage insurance when required

The site compares these costs with the cost to rent, including actual rent and renter's insurance. This site compares of the average list price of homes (adjusted for the costs above) with the average yearly rent of two bedroom apartments, condominiums, and townhomes.

Price-to-Rent = Cost to Own / Rent (annual)

$100,000 Cost / $8400 ($700/month rent) = 11.9 Price-to-Rent

According to Trulia, there are three recommendations based on this number:

- Price-to-rent 1 to 15 – much better to buy
- Price-to-Rent 16 to 20 – usually better to rent than to buy
- Price-to-Rent 21 or higher – much better to rent than to buy

Zillow.com is another real estate search site, and using a similar approach, Zillow's results are in the same ballpark, but a little lower. According to Zillow, when home prices peaked, the price-to-rent ratio nationally averaged 18.5. From 1989 to 2003, the ratio averaged about 10 nationally.

At the time this was written, Zillow showed five cities with ratios below 10, running from 5.6 to 9.2. Those cities were:

- Detroit
- Miami-Fort Lauderdale
- Dallas-Fort Worth
- Atlanta
- Phoenix

In those cities the ratio indicated that it would be better to buy a home than to rent one. However, at the same time the average would-be buyer couldn't get a mortgage or didn't have the 20% down payment most lenders required. Of course, low prices and higher rents that make these low ratios are great for investors. They can buy inexpensive properties and lease them for great ROI at market rents.

You can see the similarity between P/E and P-to-R ratios. On one side is the cost to own the asset. On the other side is the income generated by the asset. So, for the stock market investor, a high P/E means lower income per share. For the real estate investor, a higher P-to-R ratio means lower rent income in relation to the cost of the asset.

Present Value of a Future Cash Flow

When we're investing, we have a great many choices as to where to put our money. Each possible choice has its own merits and risks, and our goal is to safely invest for the best return with the lowest risk. So, we look at various similar investments to the one we're considering. We look at other real estate properties that are similar and pose similar risk/reward ratios, and we see the returns those properties generate for their investor owners.

And, we know that there are a number of properties out there that could work for us, and the numbers show that we should expect to achieve a 10% return on the property we're considering, or move on to another that can produce that rate safely.

Now we have one number we need, that 10% desired return. We're evaluating a rental property investment, and we're going to project our rental income out over the length of time we expect to own it. However, we're also going to estimate the appreciation in value we expect, so we'll estimate the amount we'll sell it for at the end of the holding period.

We realize that our annual rents don't all come in at the end of each year, but it would unnecessarily complicate the process to try and do these type of calculations on a monthly basis. So, we would come up with our anticipated annual income from rents for the number of years we expect to hold the property.

Let's say that we expect to hold a certain rent property for 5 years. We also anticipate that it will be worth approximately $152,000 at the end of that 5 years, and we'll sell it for that. Our NOI or cash flow from the property is anticipated to be:

Year 1 = $4800

Year 2 = $4200

Year 3 = $4200

Year 4 = $4500

Year 5 = $4600

Total income for five year period projected to be $22,300. We expect to receive $152,000 on sale, so the total of those two numbers is $174,300 in cash flow coming in.

Now we can determine what we're willing to pay for the property based on that 10% we found above that we want to earn. To determine what we're willing to pay we go to a Present Value Chart, which you can find in books or all over the Web with a search. Here's part of one:

Period	1%	2%	3%	4%	5%	6%	7%	8%	9%	10%	11%	12%	13%	14%	15%
1	0.990	0.980	0.971	0.962	0.952	0.943	0.935	0.926	0.917	0.909	0.901	0.893	0.885	0.877	0.870
2	0.980	0.961	0.943	0.925	0.907	0.890	0.873	0.857	0.842	0.826	0.812	0.797	0.783	0.769	0.756
3	0.971	0.942	0.915	0.889	0.864	0.840	0.816	0.794	0.772	0.751	0.721	0.712	0.693	0.675	0.658
4	0.961	0.924	0.888	0.855	0.823	0.792	0.763	0.735	0.708	0.683	659	0.636	0.613	0.592	0.572
5	0.951	0.906	0.863	0.822	0.784	0.747	0.713	0.681	0.650	0.621	0.593	0.567	0.543	0.519	0.497
6	0.942	0.888	0.837	0.790	0.746	0.705	0.666	0.630	0.596	0.564	0.535	0.507	0.480	0.456	0.432
7	0.933	0.871	0.813	0.760	0.711	0.665	0.623	0.583	0.547	0.513	0.482	0.452	0.425	0.400	0.376
8	0.923	0.853	0.789	0.731	0.677	0.627	0.582	0.540	0.502	0.467	0.434	0.404	0.376	0.351	0.327
9	0.914	0.837	0.766	0.703	0.645	0.592	0.544	0.500	0.460	0.424	0.391	0.361	0.333	0.308	0.284
10	0.905	0.820	0.744	0.676	0.614	0.558	0.508	0.463	0.422	0.386	0.352	0.322	0.295	0.270	0.247
11	0.896	0.804	0.722	0.650	0.585	0.527	0.475	0.429	0.388	0.350	0.317	0.287	0.261	0.237	0.215
12	0.887	0.788	0.701	0.625	0.557	0.497	0.444	0.397	0.356	0.319	0.286	0.257	0.231	0.208	0.187
13	0.879	0.773	0.681	0.601	0.530	0.469	0.415	0.368	0.326	0.290	0.258	0.229	0.204	0.182	0.163
14	0.870	0.758	0.661	0.577	0.505	0.442	0.388	0.340	0.299	0.263	0.232	0.205	0.181	0.160	0.141
15	0.861	0.743	0.642	0.555	0.481	0.417	0.362	0.315	0.275	0.239	0.209	0.183	0.160	0.140	0.123
16	0.853	0.728	0.623	0.534	0.458	0.394	0.339	0.292	0.252	0.218	0.188	0.163	0.141	0.123	0.107
17	0.844	0.714	0.605	0.513	0.436	0.371	0.317	0.270	0.231	0.198	0.170	0.146	0.125	0.108	0.093
18	0.836	0.700	0.587	0.494	0.416	0.350	0.296	0.250	0.212	0.180	0.153	0.130	0.111	0.095	0.081
19	0.828	0.686	0.570	0.475	0.396	0.331	0.277	0.232	0.194	0.164	0.138	0.116	0.098	0.083	0.070
20	0.820	0.673	0.554	0.456	0.377	0.312	0.258	0.215	0.178	0.149	0.124	0.104	0.087	0.073	0.061
25	0.780	0.610	0.478	0.375	0.295	0.233	0.184	0.146	0.116	0.092	0.074	0.059	0.047	0.038	0.030
30	0.742	0.552	0.412	0.308	0.231	0.174	0.131	0.099	0.075	0.057	0.044	0.033	0.026	0.020	0.015
35	0.706	0.500	0.355	0.253	0.181	0.130	0.094	0.068	0.049	0.036	0.026	0.019	0.014	0.010	0.008
40	0.672	0.453	0.307	0.208	0.142	0.097	0.067	0.046	0.032	0.022	0.015	0.011	0.008	0.005	0.004
50	0.608	0.372	0.228	0.141	0.087	0.054	0.034	0.021	0.013	0.009	0.005	0.003	0.002	0.001	0.001

To determine the Present Value of this future cash flow, we go to the Present Value Chart, go down the 10% return line to the 5 year line. Here we get a multiplier of 0.621. This is what we multiply times the future cash flow value of $174,300.

Present Value = Factor from Chart x Future Value

0.621 x $174,300 = $108,240, the Present Value

So, to realize our desired 10% return in future cash flow, we're only willing to pay up to $108,240 for this rental property to make it competitive with other investments we have available to us.

Chapter 5

6 Must-Know Real Estate Investment Methods

At the time this is being written, housing and mortgage news is still on the bad side. Lenders are still tight with their money, mortgages tough to get, and down payment requirements are up.

The really good news for investors is that this is creating a nation or renters in the near to intermediate future, or maybe longer. Real estate investors who know the strategies and techniques we'll share with you here are not looking around seeing problems.

They're seeing targets of opportunity all around them.

Sure, financing is tough. Many investors are stymied because they can't find financing to take advantage of low prices, low interest rates and higher demand for rental units.

Yes, appraisers are making everyone mad. New rules are causing appraisers to over-react in many cases, placing too much emphasis or too little on the foreclosure next door.

Money talks, but Cash screams. Buying opportunities are expected to be around for quite a while, as foreclosure pipelines are full and the process has slowed to a crawl in many areas. Buyers with cash are able to dictate terms and be very picky about the properties they buy.

In this chapter we'll look at seven ways in which investors are taking advantage of the situation and targeting blue-chip properties for long term buy and hold cash flow investing. These are techniques for 1 to 4 unit investors, the segment of the market in which the greatest opportunity exists.

We're going to give you an example for each of these methods, and it will be the same typical home in Memphis, TN. It appraises for around $100,000 by the sales comparison approach with these characteristics:

- 3 bedrooms, 2 baths
- car storage
- newer than 1978
- minimum appraisal of $75,000
- minimum rent of $750/month

Method 1: Traditional Real Estate Investment

Traditional Investment Purchase

Purchase Price	$75,000
Recent Appraisal	$100,000
Repairs Needed	none
Rented	$950

Financial Scenario

20% Down-payment	$15,000
Closing Costs	$4,500
Total Invested	$19.500
Amount Financed	$60,000
Base Mortgage PMT	$339

Total Invested	**$19.500**
Positive Cash Flow	**$200-300**
Cash on Cash Return	**12-18%**

The majority of real estate transactions are completed in this way. The buyer purchases an improved rental home with a 20% down payment, financing the property with a fixed 30-year mortgage.

According to a popular and reliable investment survey, the average transaction is one completed with a $28,000 down payment from the investor. This method is still in favor with lenders and has changed little in the last few turbulent years.

The home of course must appraise to the purchase price, but many investors are still able to purchase improved properties at nice discounts for investments with good cash flow.

Pros

The long term low interest rate is the first advantage. It's one of the easiest mortgages to get. Even with 20% down, decent returns and good cash flows can be achieved.

Cons

It's a qualifying loan, so a great credit score is required. Assets are scrutinized, and investors are paying more because the properties must me in appraisable condition.

Method 2: Limited Cash Investment

While pre-2007 this type of purchase was very common, in fact courted by lenders, it's a whole different story now. While money can be found to make these deals, it's becoming more difficult, and appraisals are a problem as well.

The goal here is to purchase a home in need of repairs and improvements at a deep discount. A short-term lender's money is used to complete the purchase and renovations.

That short-term high cost loan is then refinanced with a 30-year fixed rate loan with a regular permanent lender. When it works, the investor

Limited Investment Purchase

Purchase Price	$60,000
Recent Appraisal	$100,000
Repairs Needed	$10,000
Future Rental	$950

Financial Scenario (Loan 1)

Purchase/Improvement	$70,000
Closing Costs & Points	$5,000
Down Payment	$5,000
Amount Financed	$70,000
Short Term PMT	$700

Refinance in 90 Days

30 Year Loan Amount	$75,000
Closing Costs & Points	$5,000
Additional Invested	$7,000
Amount Financed	$75,000
30 Year Base PMT	$435

Total Invested	$12,000
Positive Cash Flow	$100-200
Cash on Cash Return	10-20%

is able to buy the property with roughly 5% to 15% invested, though that's dependent upon the permanent lender's appraised value.

Pros

As you can see in the example numbers breakdown, this is a potentially high return, low cash strategy. Many buyers are managing to leverage other people's money and get into these deals with as little as $5000 cash invested. It's a creative way to beat the 20% down system.

Cons

The cost of the short term loan is high, and the appraisal is a big unknown, sometimes ruining the best laid plans of the investor. Appraisals have been known to double that expected $5000 figure.

Method 3: Line of Credit

Line of Credit Purchase

Purchase Price	$80,000
Recent Appraisal	$100,000
Repairs Needed	none
Amount Financed	$80,000
Base Monthly PMT	$333

Unimproved

Down-payment	$60,000
Recent Appraisal	$100,000
Repairs Needed	$10,000
Amount Financed	$70,000
Base Mortgage PMT	$291

Total Invested	$0
Positive Cash Flow	$200-350
Cash on Cash Return	$$$

While banks almost stopped making HELOC (Home Equity Line of Credit) loans and other equity line loans for a while after 2006, they're beginning to show up again and gaining ground.

When an amazing opportunity to buy a great property at rock-bottom pricing is staring an investor in the face, the HELOC or line of credit loan can be the way to make it happen.

Because this can be set up in advance before you need it, when the right property is located the negotiation goes quickly, as it's much the same as a cash deal with the funds readily available.

The banks usually offer an interest only payment option as well. This can increase cash flow at the front end of the investment which is a nice result.

Pros

The line of credit is established in advance, so there aren't loan qualification issues when a property is located, and there can be a quick closing process allowing for a stronger buyer negotiation position. Interest payments are tax deductible, and interest only payments may be offered.

Cons

They're tougher loans to get these days, but still out there. This is really a short term solution as there is no amortization.

Method 4: IRA Investment

How's your outlook for drawing Social Security? It's not looking good for a large chunk of the populace, with government deficits and raids on the Social Security piggy bank to fund government. More people are looking at other ways to secure their retirement, and the IRA, Individual Retirement Account is one of the favorites.

Regular brokerages don't usually offer self-directed IRA investment in real estate, as they'd rather sell stocks and mutual funds for commissions. However, higher demand lately has created a supply response, and companies like Guidant Financial, Entrust, Equity Trust, and others are offering real estate investment in IRA accounts.

The investor locates the properties for investment and the transaction is run through the IRA, usually as a full cash real estate purchase. A few special characteristics attach to this type of investing:

IRA Purchase

Improved

Purchase Price	$80,000
Recent Appraisal	$100,000
Repairs Needed	none
Amount Financed	none

Unimproved

Down-payment	$60,000
Recent Appraisal	$100,000
Repairs Needed	$10,000
Amount Financed	none

Total Invested	**$70-80,000**
Positive Cash Flow	**$500-650**
Cash on Cash Return	**8-11%**

- The home is purchased in the name of the IRA.
- All funds, in or out, MUST run through the IRA.
- Rents and expenses funnel through the account.
- Some IRA brokerages set up checkbook accounts to simplify the payment of expenses and give the investor more control.
- This also cuts some of the management duties and therefore costs associated with this type of account.
- Costs to the investor can include setup, transaction and ongoing management fees.

All the buyer needs to do once the IRA is set up is to provide the seller with a proof-of-funds statement from the IRA, and the transaction flows through like it's a cash deal.

Pros

The buyer is in a good negotiating position as this type of deal is similar to a cash transaction and can close quickly. Proceeds, including net income and appreciation at sale, are either tax-deferred or tax free in the case of a Roth IRA. It's easy to roll over a traditional IRA to a self-directed account.

Cons

One must be very careful to follow all of the IRS rules and abide by restrictions or severe penalties can result. Transactions must be arms-length. Transaction and ongoing fees can be high.

Method 5: Cash Purchase

Cash Purchase

Improved

Purchase Price	$80,000
Recent Appraisal	$100,000
Repairs Needed	none
Amount Financed	none

Unimproved

Down-payment	$60,000
Recent Appraisal	$100,000
Repairs Needed	$10,000
Amount Financed	none

Total Invested	$70-80,000
Positive Cash Flow	$500-650
Cash on Cash Return	8-11%

In several areas of this book we talk about leverage, and using other people's money to invest in real estate. And, it's a viable strategy for a huge number of investors. There's nothing wrong with leverage if used properly.

However, buying with cash can in many cases be the very best way to invest in real estate. Cash buyers have the ultimate in negotiating power. Cash buyers close faster and cash flow is maximized when there's no mortgage payment.

Of course, there is the other side of that coin, the loss of tax advantages of the mortgage interest deduction and the opportunity to increase net worth with leverage. However, cash investors will argue that they always get the best prices.

Pros

Closings come in a hurry, cash flow is highest, and the buyer has a great negotiation advantage.

Cons

Cash is a finite resource, so leverage could be a better course. Cash buyers miss the tax advantages of deducting mortgage interest and financial costs.

Method 6: Equity Participation

Equity Participation Purchase

Total Invested	$50-500,000
Cash on Cash Return	10%+

- Multiple Options, Tailored Approach
- Can participate as lendor only or participate in equity

For a great many investors, it can be more desirable to participate in equity and cash flow but not in the day-to-day management of properties. These investors provide money as partners, while other experienced investors take the hands-on part of the deals.

There are a great many ways to structure equity partnerships. However, the common thread in all is that the equity investor puts up a lump sum of cash and then receives their return on investment through some cash flow and an equity stake when the property is sold.

Pros

The investor enjoys many of the advantages of real estate investment without day-to-day involvement, indeed not communicating with managing investors at all in many cases. There's a lot of flexibility in the formation of these partnerships.

Cons

Because the active partners normally participate at a higher percentage of ownership, the equity partners receive smaller returns than they would in other types of deals.

Summing Up

There's a lot of math wrapped up in real estate investing, but that doesn't mean it's a science. There's some art to real estate investing as well. Between economic trends, government intervention, and human nature, investing in real estate involves a great many factors and creates a moving target for success.

The methods we've just shared with you are all effective at times for some investors, and they may not work at times for others. Real estate investing is interesting and never dull, because of these factors.

Chapter 6

Leverage Rewards and Risk

Leverage is using borrowed money to increase a real estate portfolio's size and to increase the return on cash invested. Most of the articles you'll find on Web searches for "real estate investment leverage" will look on it favorably, as it's been a really great tool for building wealth for a great many real estate investors.

Other articles will take a much more conservative approach and speak to the risks of leverage, even in an investment as secure as real estate. This is particularly true of any articles referencing the drop in home values that began in earnest in 2007 after the crash of the housing and mortgage markets. Many real estate investors took huge hits to their portfolios and net worth, and some went under, losing their properties to foreclosure.

So, which is the more "realistic" view of leverage in real estate? Actually, it's a balance of both.

What Happened to the Investors Who Lost?

Many investors did run into real trouble starting in 2007, and unless other financial situations took them down, they were in general "over-leveraged" in real estate. Their purchase decisions and market analysis and planning weren't conservative enough to carry them through what would be a temporary, though years long, situation.

They Weren't Blue-chip Investors

The majority of the real estate investors who lost properties during this period to foreclosure were not blue-chip investors. They combined leverage and low-priced properties to build larger portfolios and increase cash-on-cash return. However, many of their properties were returning low cash flows that were sufficient to hold them unless vacancies, turnover, and credit losses increased ... which they did for many during this period.

While real estate was increasing in value, some of these investors even borrowed on equity in their longer hold properties to purchase others. This ran up their costs on the older properties, cut cash flow, and became a real problem when the market turned.

Blue-chip properties are those that draw a more stable tenant, those who value the neighborhoods and schools and are likely to stay in the rental longer. When turnover and vacancies drop, profits rise, and there's less risk in leverage with blue-chips.

Their Strategies Invited Risk

There's a whole lot of real estate investor training and advisory material out there that leads the investor to low-priced properties that can command high returns on cash invested through leverage. In Chapter 3 we looked at how a penny property purchase can go from a double-digit return to less than half due to vacancy and credit losses more common to lower end properties.

The losing investors in many cases also failed to thoroughly research their markets, instead buying in neighborhoods saturated with tenants and vacancies. When local businesses began to suffer and lay off employees or close their doors, people moved away for jobs, increasing vacancy rates. Others stayed, but with lower priced jobs or unemployment, their ability to pay rent suffered, running up credit losses for investors.

When situations begin to deteriorate in an area, landlords lower rent to compete for poorer and fewer tenants, and this is when leverage can wipe out cash flow. When investors begin to have to pay out of pocket every month, things go downhill fast.

Local Governments Made it Worse

In many areas, the poor economy forced local governments to raise property tax rates while not lowering values to true market levels. Property taxes are a direct out-of-pocket expense, and for many penny property investors, tax increases dramatically cut their return on investment.

Real Estate or Stock Market Investment

To illustrate the value of leverage in real estate, let's look at $100,000 invested in real estate versus the same investment in buying and holding a stock. We'll not use stock market leverage, as it's really not a viable strategy when the stock broker holds all of the cards and will automatically sell your investment when you can't respond to a margin call with more cash. This will be a comparison of a straight cash stock purchase and a real estate purchase with financing.

Description	Real Estate	Stock
Initial Value	$100,000	$100,000
Amount Invested*	$24,000	$0
Mortgage or margin amount	$80,000	$0
Mortgage or margin interest**	6%	0%
Projected annual growth***	3%	8%
Projected value in 10 years****	$134,392	$215,893
Projected profit at sale*****	$34,392	$115,893

*20% down payment and $4000 closing costs.

**Note: Informational, as we're paying this out of our cash flow with a profit.

***Note: 3% conservative estimate for real estate appreciation. Stock is high-growth with 8%, thus pays no dividends.

****Note: From compound rate table, with compounding once each year.

*****Note: Costs of sale not included for simplicity of comparison, but real estate would carry a higher percentage of resale cost. However, if rolling the sale into another purchase with a 1031 exchange, some of the cost difference would be offset because capital gains would be avoided on real estate but must be paid on the stock sale.

While our stock investment returned almost 116% on the cash invested, the real estate investment returned approximately 143% in resale profit alone on the $24,000 invested and leveraged.

Keep in mind that we did not take into account the monthly positive cash flow generated for 10 years; a really large return on investment.

The mortgage payment would have been $480/month. With taxes and insurance, about $660, and this property would probably rent for around $900/month.

Even if we could have gotten a dividend and the 8% return from the stock investment, it would have been eclipsed by adding the resale profits to the monthly cash flow in the real estate deal.

Let's not over-simplify this to the point of being misleading. There are definitely a number of costs of ownership of real estate that aren't involved with the negligible cost of holding stocks in an investment account.

- Mortgage interest
- Property taxes
- Home insurance
- Repair and maintenance
- Other management costs

However, when we're working with blue-chip properties, we've only purchased with the knowledge that we can produce a positive annual return over and above these expenses through our rental income. Plus, we can also benefit from tax deductions and depreciation.

Real Estate Leverage Comparison

In a previous chapter we discussed leverage a bit, but let's get into it just a bit more here. First, we'll be purchasing a blue-chip investment property in a high demand area with good schools, stable business and a growing economy. We'll not be taking into account any credit losses or other issues, as we want this to be a simple comparison of return based on the amount leveraged. The property:

- 100,000 home for rental investment
- Financing with a mortgage at 5.5% interest for 30 years
- $2900 annual expenses for insurance, taxes and repairs

- Rental income of $1000/month
- ½ month vacancy each year, or $500
- Added to expenses, becomes $3400 total expenses

Let's run through four different down payment options for this investment.

$100,000 paid in full, no down payment or leverage

- $12,000 in rental income - $3400 expenses = $8600 NOI
- no mortgage payments or interest
- $8,600 / $100,000 = .086 or **8.6% ROI** on cash invested

$50,000 invested as 50% down, $50,000 financed

- $12,000 in rental income - $3400 expenses = $8600 NOI
- $284 monthly payment x 12 = $3408 annual
- $8600 - $3408 = $5192 / $50,000 invested = **10.3% ROI**

$20,000 invested as 20% down, $80,000 financed

- $12,000 in rental income - $3400 expenses = $8600 NOI
- $454 monthly payment x 12 = $5448 annual
- $8600 - $5448 = $3152 / $20,000 invested = **15.7% ROI**

$10,000 invested as 10% down, $90,000 financed

- $12,000 in rental income - $3400 expenses = $8600 NOI
- $511 monthly payment x 12 = $6132 annual
- $8600 – 6132 = $2468 / $10,000 invested = **24.7% ROI**

From these examples we can see that our percentage return on cash invested climbs steeply the less we put into the purchase. However, let's look at just one component of risk that must be considered and will definitely influence our decision.

Our cash flow drops considerably as our return climbs in these examples. Let's make an assumption that there are economic conditions that follow our placement of this property into rental service, and they result in this situation:

- Higher than anticipated vacancy reduces our income on average by an extra month or $1000, we must reduce rent to $850/month on average, and expenses & taxes rise by $100/month, bringing our NOI to an average of $5100/year.

Now let's run the situations above for the three situations with a mortgage.

$50,000 invested as 50% down, $50,000 financed

- $,5100 NOI
- $284 monthly payment x 12 = $3408 annual
- $5100 - $2908 = $2192 / $50,000 invested = **4.3% ROI**

$20,000 invested as 20% down, $80,000 financed

- $5,100 NOI
- $454 monthly payment x 12 = $5448 annual
- $5100 - $5448 = $(348) / $20,000 invested = **(1.7%) ROI**

$10,000 invested as 10% down, $90,000 financed

- $5,100 NOI
- $511 monthly payment x 12 = $6132 annual
- $5100 – 6132 = ($1032) / $10,000 invested = **(10.3%) ROI**

In reality, it can often get worse. None of these situations take into account precipitous drops in value and the possibility the investor may be forced to try and sell and take a loss, or lose the home to foreclosure.

4 Real Estate Leverage Don'ts

1. **Don't count on past history for appreciation** – You see
    this warning all the time in relation to investing in the
    stock market: "Past history is not necessarily an indicator
    of future performance." Lock in some profit up front as a
    discount to existing value by negotiating a bargain
    purchase price. Appreciation after that can be predicted
    but shouldn't be relied upon for a profitable investment.
2. **Don't forget to balance down payment with cash flow
    intelligently** – a low down payment might look good at
    first glance, but higher payments will be around through
    the entire ownership period and could put your cash flow
    into too risky of a position.
3. **Don't regard super financing as always the best
    approach** – this is a leverage issue but also a future risk
    issue. If you take out creative financing, maybe a short
    period ARM to maximize cash flow at the beginning of
    your ownership, you could end up having to refinance at
    a much higher rate sooner than desired. This can be
    devastating to cash flow.

4. **Never forget that cash flow is king** – we've gone through a calculation to determine present value from a stream of future income, and that calculation uses a projected sale amount and profit at sale. However, the ultimate real value of a rental property is in the monthly positive cash flow that gets deposited into your bank account.

6 Real Estate Leverage Dos

1. **Look for below market rents if rented** – sometimes you'll confront an opportunity to purchase a property that's been in rental service, and even comes with a tenant in place. Look for one with below market rent being charged, as it influences the seller's idea of value, could get you a better deal, and will allow you to raise the rent at lease end to increase your ROI.
2. **Creative financing can be a good thing** – now and then a property can be purchased with an assumption. Or, sometimes an ARM, Adjustable Rate Mortgage, can work to increase cash flow. When you can cut the interest rate significantly with a five or seven year ARM, and you

don't plan to hold the home longer than that, it's a good decision.

3. **Just make a higher down payment** – this is a chapter about leverage, so always consider a higher down payment if it reduces risk and can still provide a good return on your investment.

4. **Improvable properties can be great investments** – some properties lend themselves well to modernization remodeling or to additions to increase the size and rents. This size decision is especially valuable in college markets where roommates share rent.

5. **Look for the hot or in-demand areas** – we mention this a lot in relation to blue-chip investments. In-demand areas for families almost always have excellent school systems which keep them in occupancy longer for higher profits.

6. **Always be buying value** – always be trying to lock in your profit on the front end. Appreciation should be a bonus. Buy below true market value to start out with instant equity.

How Blue-chips Increase Leverage at Lower Risk

Now that we've thoroughly quantified the value of careful leverage and the risks of careless leverage, how does this blue-chip investing strategy fit in?

The blue-chip real estate investment strategy requires a careful analysis of the local market to determine the very best areas in which to buy. Stable areas that have a history of demand, as well as growth areas are both good candidates. Excellent school systems draw families as tenants, and they stay longer. Sometimes they charge higher taxes, but you'll determine if you can still get the cash flow you want from rents you can charge.

The best neighborhoods reduce the risk that comes with leverage, as rents are more stable, and investors can usually raise rents enough to offset inflation. These neighborhoods also normally provide a higher appreciation rate, so more profit at resale.

Repairs and maintenance, especially the unexpected, bring risk to real estate investment. Buying blue-chip properties reduces that risk substantially. Selecting only properties in excellent condition and newer in age will reduce repair and maintenance expenses over time and help you to avoid major unexpected expenses.

Blue-chip properties normally appreciate at higher rates over time. Neighborhoods in demand always command higher prices, especially when the areas are static in size and the number of available properties is finite.

Leverage carries risk, but it also carries amazing growth potential for your net worth and cash flow. Learning to use it wisely will make a major difference in your real estate investment results.

Chapter 7

Market Trends &
Recovery Expectations

The housing and mortgage market crash that started taking shape seriously in 2007 continued through 2011 and was predicted at that time to be a situation that would hang around into 2013 or later years. Whenever you're reading this, the effects are actually expected to last much longer. Why?

The financial situation in our government is one that is moving toward eliminating or drastically curtailing government involvement in guaranteeing home loans. Even programs that may continue will only want to back the strongest of borrowers, or will charge ever higher fees to offset risk.

Lenders became severely restrictive in regards to mortgage lending post-2007, and the trend continues. Higher down payments, better credit scores, and excruciating scrutiny of all income and expenses is expected to be the norm "into the foreseeable future" according to Morgan Stanley in a report issued in late 2011.

Big Players Seeing a New Market in Single Family Rentals

The title of the Morgan Stanley report is "Housing Market Insights A Rentership Society." For a large financial institution to use phrases like "foreseeable future" when referring to the inability of people to get mortgages, it's clear that times have changed a lot in America.

The major focus of the report was to inform their investors of opportunities never before present in this country for large institutions to break into the single family rental market. New REITs, Real Estate Investment Trusts, are forming to take advantage of this "perfect storm" in U.S. housing trends.

The report states that the single family home rental market in the past has been dominated by individual and small investors. Reasons for this include the inability of large institutions to amass enough properties in locations where they could be adequately managed for profit.

Things are certainly different now. In fact, the government has tentatively broached the idea of mass liquidations of Freddie Mac and Fannie Mae properties to institutions and mega-investors. In the past there wasn't enough ability to purchase single family homes at prices that would create enough room for management costs and profits that would suit investors in REITs and large institutional portfolios.

The volume of distressed properties is now such that large volume purchases by these big players can be made at such bargain basement prices that profits are guaranteed. With the resources these companies bring to the table, buying, rehabbing and managing these properties can be profitable like never before in history.

Some would ask if this is a trend that's going to be around for a while. That "foreseeable future" quote indicated that this country should be a rentership society for many years to come. While a quick look at the homeownership rate in this country in the 65% range might make one wonder, the fact is that if you take out the people in homes in the foreclosure process, more than 2 million right now, American homeownership would be the lowest ever tracked since the 1930s at around 59.7%.

From the cover page of the report, a few bullet points:

- *"The combination of falling home prices, limited mortgage credit, continued liquidations, and better rental options is fundamentally changing the way Americans live."*

- *"Including delinquent borrowers, the homeownership rate, which officially stands at 66.4%, would instead be 59.7%."*
- *"The demand for shelter is growing, but the lack of mortgage credit will drive this demand to the rental market at the expense of the owner occupied market."*
- *"Each distressed single-family liquidation creates a potential renter household, as well as a potential single-family rental unit."*

The next question that arises is about the increased construction of apartment units that was already beginning to develop in 2011. Why won't apartments absorb the majority of this new rental demand? Some will go there, but data shows that apartment renters tend to be more transient and younger. Those with families who have children and want good schools will want to live in the same type of homes they lost to foreclosure, and in the same neighborhoods.

It's About the Total Market for Shelter

Morgan Stanley took a somewhat different approach to evaluating the market in terms of owner occupied or rental properties. They chose to consider the entire market, both owner occupied and rental properties and look at supply and demand. Their take is that the underlying fundamentals are increasingly positive if you look at the market in terms of supply and demand for "shelter", whatever the type or ownership.

Household Formations

The formation of new households has always been a housing market-driver, though in the past it was mostly measured in terms of demand for buying homes. While historic data shows that the rate of new household formation typically lags during recessions, it's been steadily improving since the Great Depression.

And, while there is a lot of data out currently showing home ownership rates akin to those during the Depression, it's more of a result of loose mortgage rules and the frenzy to buy that died at the end of 2006. New household formation is still happening, families are forming, and children are coming into the world.

The demand for shelter in this country is increasing, but the supply is being absorbed at an increasing rate. Concentrating on the entire sector, both single family and multi-family, excess units are declining. Builders all but ceased activities starting in 2007, and lending is still tight for builders as well as buyers.

Some analysts predict that any signs of improvement will bring a rush to construction, but the shortage is not going to go away overnight, and Americans have a different mindset these days. They aren't seeing owning a home in the same light as just a few short years ago.

The Owner/Renter Divide

The previous views of homeownership, that it's a great investment, and that home values will always rise, are no longer held by the majority of the population. We're moving from an ownership society to a rentership society and the reports gives four fundamental reasons for this trend:

1. Lenders have tightened borrower credit and qualification requirements and raised down payments to the point that mortgage lending has almost stopped.
2. The fall of home prices in just about every area of the country for a sustained period is deflating the desirability of homeownership. Potential buyers simply do not want to risk buying into a falling market.
3. Mortgage delinquencies, foreclosures and liquidations continue to turn massive numbers of homeowners into renters. Demand for rental units is climbing as a result.
4. For the first time in history, the government is quiet about home ownership, not promoting it as the "American Dream." There is also a scaling back of government guarantees and direct home buyer incentives.

As for item 4, here's a direct quote from the U.S. Treasury:

"In the past, the government's financial and tax policies encouraged housing purchases and real estate investment over other sectors of our economy, and ultimately left taxpayers responsible for much of the risk incurred by a poorly supervised housing finance market."

"The Administration believes that we must continue to take the necessary steps to ensure that Americans have access to an adequate range of affordable housing options. This does not mean our goal is for all Americans to be homeowners."

You're No Longer "Throwing Your Money Away"

The mantra of the National Association of Realtors and many others for 30+ years has been that owning a home is your best investment and that you're throwing your money away if you rent. However, renting is no longer tarnished, and is gaining ground because it's necessary as an option when buying isn't possible, and due to the many homes in distress.

While it's easy to gather data about multi-family rentals, the single family market is much more fragmented due to the type of investors involved. They don't report to a central data-gathering organization, so it's more difficult to track the single family rental market.

The multi-family rental market began a comeback in 2010, and was considered as booming in 2011. However, the new "tenant" profile is a game-changer when it comes to comparing multi-family with single family rental trends.

- The new "tenants" are much more likely to be former homeowners who value stability and neighborhoods with good schools, as well as homes with yards and privacy.
- The new "tenants" want to remain close to where they lived and live in a home much like the one they lost.

This is changing the demand profile for rental units. It's definitely trending to single family homes, and mostly in better neighborhoods. This further supports the blue-chip investment strategy.

How Long Will This Trend Last?

Until unemployment and the overall economy improve, and until access to credit eases, it's considered that this movement toward a rentership society will continue. One more quote from the Morgan Stanley report:

"Specifically, GSE reform, Dodd-Frank securitization rules, mortgage interest deduction reform, continued home price declines and a long workout period for distressed homes, will likely make it harder to buy an owner-occupied home. As such, we believe that the US will become a Rentership Society, in which the homeownership rate will keep falling, the home rentership rate will conversely rise, and the rental market will dominate the investment landscape in housing for years to come."

In an article from the Wall Street Journal, there's a story of a construction worker from the San Francisco bay area. He lost his job in 2009, and 10 months later lost his home to foreclosure.

A father of four, he now rents that same five-bedroom home from McKinley Capital Partners, an investment company moving into the single family rental home market. More and more hedge funds and private equity firms are doing the same. Having purchased more than 300 single family homes in the Bay Area in 209 into 2011, McKinley is partnering up with another company with plans to buy 500 more in a 2 year period.

The opportunities are out there, with almost four million homes in some stage of default or foreclosure at the end of 2011. And, with the foreclosure process taking a year or more in many states, the supply should be there for some time to come. And, for every foreclosure there's a tenant wanting a nice place to rent.

Like Three Large Weather Fronts Converging, It's a Perfect Storm

1. Front 1: Real estate prices are severely discounted and great cash flows from rentals are the result.
2. Real estate is stable and tangible. Investors want tangible goods to secure their investments.
3. We're trending from an ownership society to a rentership populace.

Never before has a blue-chip real estate investment strategy been so available to the average investor. The institutions and big capital conglomerates know it, and now you do too.

Chapter 8

The Rare Event Horizon

Whether you call it a "perfect storm" or a "rare event horizon," it's when seemingly unrelated events come together to produce an outsized response. The response can be terrible, as in a "perfect storm" brought about when weather fronts converge. Or, it can be an amazing situation when financial and economic events converge to bring about huge opportunity.

This chapter's goal is to explain "Cause and Effect," or in this case "Cause and Opportunity." Understanding what's happening in the U.S. housing and mortgage markets, and treating those happenings as causes, we can draw conclusions as to the opportunities that should result from the events.

Cause: Record Low Interest Rates

Courtesy: *'Reproduced with the permission of Mortgage-X.com'*

Interest rates in 2011 hovered at 30 year historic lows. Dipping under 4% on multiple occasions for a 30 year fixed rate, the news should have been outstanding for home buyers. However, they couldn't get mortgages, so the interest rate didn't matter.

Opportunity

Real Estate rental property investors rely primarily on cash flow. That's rental income in excess of cash outflow and expenses. Part of that cash outflow is the mortgage payment. So, when interest rates are high, it can be impossible to buy an investment property with a mortgage and still realize a positive cash flow that justifies the risk and cash invested.

When interest rates are very low, the cost of borrowed money is very low as well. Mortgage payments go down, and cash flow goes up. In fact, rental property investments that would otherwise not be feasible actually become attractive.

Cause: Steep Drop in Home Prices

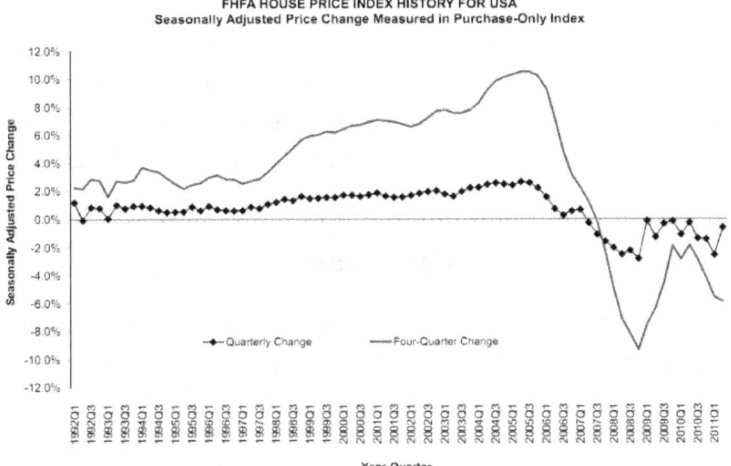

FHFA HOUSE PRICE INDEX HISTORY FOR USA
Seasonally Adjusted Price Change Measured in Purchase-Only Index

Nationally, the estimate in 2011 was that home prices had dropped on average by more than 30% from their 2006 highs. In some areas, such as Arizona and Florida, prices actually nosedived by 50% to 70%. In fact, with more than 4 million foreclosures still in the pipeline at the end of 2011, further price declines of 3% to 5% were anticipated over the next couple of years.

Opportunity

The previous item brings out that low interest rates make using other peoples' money less expensive. When the investment asset is also at bargain-basement prices, it's all the better. Couple lower cash to get into a deal because of depressed prices with lower interest rates, and cash flows skyrocket.

Cause: Record Low Home Construction

While a good graph wasn't available, the construction of new homes dropped by almost 25% in 2007 alone. Building continued to decline into 2011, when a little light was seen at the end of the tunnel. However, with no buying pressure, builders have little incentive to build homes.

New homes simply haven't been a priority for years. First time home buyers, the primary consumers of new homes in the U.S. are an endangered species. Without a reasonable expectation of a buyer at a profitable price, home builders would rather sell off assets, and sit back and wait.

Opportunity

Fully a third of the population is unable to qualify for a mortgage, and their sentiment has changed from a "must-own" view to one of just wanting to have shelter they enjoy and can afford. These factors are making quality rentals a goal for an ever-growing segment of the population.

Cause: Record Foreclosures

Record numbers of foreclosures displaced record numbers of families in the U.S. Many had been in their homes for years. They found themselves either unemployed or underwater in their mortgages and unable to sell. Losing a home to foreclosure doesn't mean that the owner is relocating, actually it's rare. Especially when jobs are tough to get, losing a home will normally not spur the owner to leave the area and take on more uncertainty in their lives.

Opportunity

Displaced homeowners need to live somewhere; they need shelter. They can't get a mortgage, but they still have a job and need a place to live. Families still want to be located in nice neighborhoods with good schools. Many want to stay in the neighborhoods where they lost their home. This creates a unique opportunity for blue-chip investors to provide rental homes in those areas.

Cause: Declining Homeownership Rates

As we discussed in the market trends chapter, home ownership rates are lower than they've been since World War II. If the number for those currently in foreclosure is subtracted, the rate is the lowest since the Great Depression. They're not in an owned home, but they're not dead either. Also, we learned that new families are being formed, but we still have lower home ownership rates.

Opportunity

This again leads us to the fact that all of these families need a home, and they are driving up the demand for quality rental properties. Investors who can provide those quality units in neighborhoods where people want to live will prosper for years into the future.

Cause: Echo Boom Population 80 Million

Echo Boomers, also known as Generation Y, are roughly defined as those born from the 1970s to the early 2000s. They have watched the events beginning in 2007, and they've seen their parents and others lose their home equity and even their homes to foreclosure. They do not have a very positive view of home ownership. Surveys show that they are content to rent for years into the future.

Opportunity

This situation and this group will simply drive up demand for rental properties even more. By focusing on blue-chip rental properties, the investor can be selective and court those with good jobs and the ability to pay rents that generate great cash flow.

From CNBC: 52% of the world's population is under the age of 30 ... the youth will be the driving force of the future of housing.

Chapter 9

The Target Blue-chip Property

What makes a property stand out as a blue-chip investment? Take the same question and apply it to the stocks and bonds in your 401k or other retirement account. The retirement investor wants stability, reasonable growth, and an acceptable risk profile. We don't want to risk our later years with speculative investments.

Retirement accounts hold stocks like Coca Cola, Walmart, Apple, and Google, not penny stocks. Bonds in retirement accounts are normally U.S. government or municipal bonds from strong economic areas, not short term Greek bonds.

Security over the long term is a major factor in portfolio decisions, and it should be no different when it comes to real estate investment. You can have the very best investment education, super property management, and a great team for renovation, but none of these rise to the level of importance of selection of the right product.

What are the major considerations in selecting that "right" product? It should be:

- easy to rent
- attractive to tenants
- low maintenance
- hold its value
- easy to sell when it's time to exit the investment

All of these characteristics combine to create a rental property investment that will experience lower than normal vacancy and credit loss, above-average market rents, and better resale potential. In this chapter we'll examine factors that influence each of these attributes in detail in order to give you a high level of confidence in your property selections.

Property Characteristics

When it comes to the characteristics that tenants look for in a property, there is a tendency to try to gather data from rentals alone. This creates data distortion, because we're assuming that what they're renting is really what they want. Too many tenants settle because they can't get what they want where they want it.

Tenants actually want the same things that buyers do. The fact that they do not want to buy, or that they can't buy, doesn't change their lifestyles nor the areas where they prefer to live. In fact, the blue-chip property investment strategy is enhanced by the fact that the investor is many times offering a property for rent that is in greater demand and lesser supply than competing properties.

G.E. Miller of *Get Rich Slowly* lists a few of the items the majority of the population search for in either a home purchase or rental:

- 3 to 4 bedrooms, with 4 normally being the upper limit
- 1.5 to 2 baths
- 1000 to 2000 square feet for comfort and efficiency
- central heat and air conditioning
- a pleasant kitchen with nice cabinets
- a garage
- energy efficiency, including windows and insulation

Though not every buyer or renter is making these characteristics requirements in their search, sharp investors will select properties that exhibit the majority of factors desired by the majority of prospects.

Lifestyles and a trend toward more work remote from the office no doubt contribute to the desire for at least 3 bedrooms, as one is many times converted to an office space. Especially in areas with large technology workforces, a great deal of telecommuting is done with the full approval and encouragement of the employer.

The cost of an automobile these days is a factor in the desire for a garage to protect it. However, garages are storage facilities and workshops as well for many. Keeping these lifestyle trends in mind when selecting properties for blue-chip investing will increase return on investment.

Neighborhood and Location

We've heard over and over that real estate is all about "location…location…location" when it comes to selling a home. It's just as true for rental properties. Location can be the single most influential characteristic in a tenant's decision to sign a lease.

Population demographics change over time, but there are areas and neighborhoods that tend to always be in-demand. Whether it's a nice rural feel that's close to the urban jobs, or an older urban area that's being rejuvenated and gentrified, there are always neighborhoods that tend to outperform others over many years.

The due diligence for blue-chip rental properties begins with neighborhood. Drilling down a bit, there can be differences between one street and another. In some high demand subdivisions, there are certain streets, perhaps those too close to busy streets or commercial areas, that just don't sell as well or command the same prices as other streets very nearby.

While homes in a cul-de-sac can be better investments, gathering past sales data can help the investor to determine if this is the case or not. Orientation of the home can make a difference, especially in colder climates. If homes on one side of the street have a better southern exposure, solar gain will make them more efficient in the winter.

Property Taxes

Property taxes can be a location issue. A prime neighborhood in most other respects can become a tougher area for cash flow, as the property taxes are too high. Also check to see if there are any initiatives published or rumored that would raise taxes significantly. This is especially true when municipalities are having budget problems.

Schools are Always a Consideration

Whenever you run into a list of top areas or concerns of home buyers or renters, schools will always be one of the priority items. The Department of Housing and Urban Development states: *"Many people choose communities based on schools."*

Remember that we've already determined that renters want pretty much the same things that home buyers do, so this from the National Association of Realtors® is important:

" Of all the local neighborhood amenities that can influence a buyer's decision to purchase a home, proximity to good quality schools is one of the most influential. According to the2010 National Association of REALTORS® Profile of Home Buyers and Sellers, 25% of home buyers listed school quality and 19% listed proximity to schools as deciding factors in their home purchase."

This is good information because it comes from asking questions of actual home buyers, and they state that schools were a "deciding factor" in their home purchase.

When you're researching a neighborhood, there are a number of websites with school location maps. Google does a good job, with this map in Albuquerque, NM as an example:

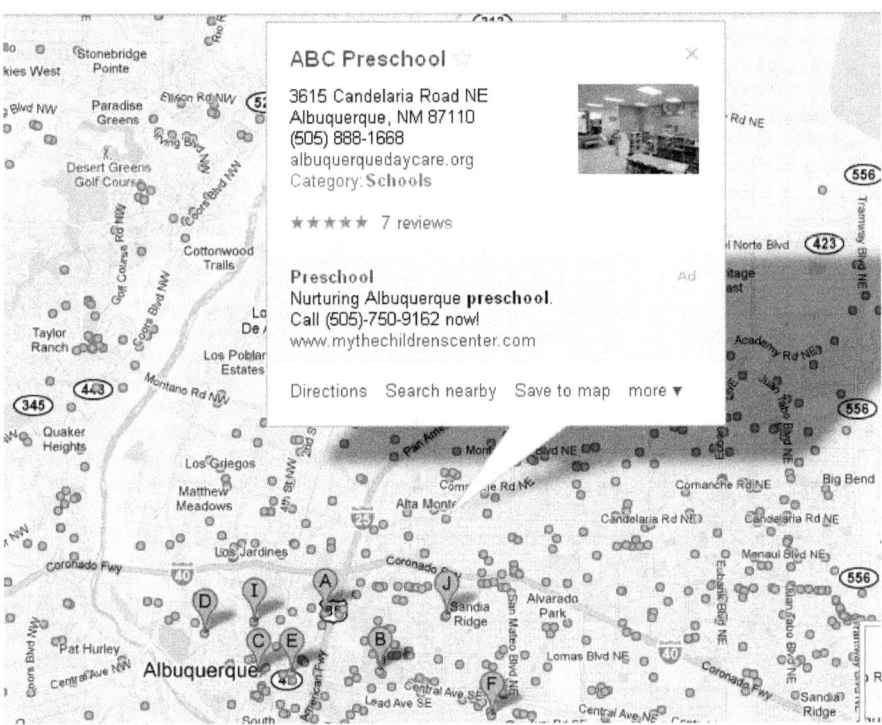

Hovering over one of the dots provides the name and type of school, but clicking on it gives a lot more data as you can see in the screen shot. Your next step would be to check out several of them on a school rating website. Here's a screen shot from GreatSchools.org for an Elementary School in Denver:

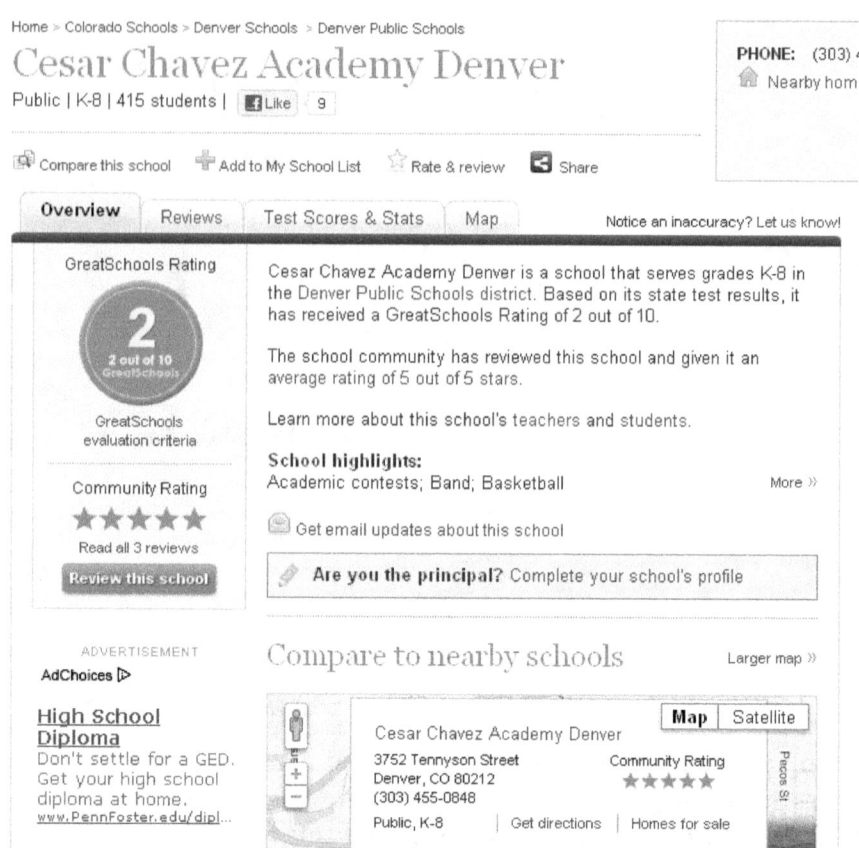

The tabs give you access to not only an overview, but reviews, test scores and statistics. In your research to locate the very best blue-chip rental properties, you'll want to map and rate the schools.

One approach is to locate properties by home and structural characteristics, then do the area, location, and schools research. On the flip side, you can do the location and school research then find suitable properties in those areas with blue-chip characteristics. Either way, these are your top three selection priorities, then move on to others we'll talk about now.

The Crime Effect

If you were considering buying a home, would you be concerned if you discovered a higher incidence of crime there than in other areas in which you could live? Of course it would be a concern, and it's no different for renters. The safety of their families is just as important to them, and they will rule out an otherwise suitable area if crime is an issue.

Crime is a threat to your tenant and their possessions, and will probably cost you money in maintenance over time ... think stolen air conditioners. The influence of crime on your cash flow should be a concern. In higher crime areas, you'll have a much more difficult task in attracting quality tenants, they'll turn over more often, and your rental income will be lower.

There are a number of online resources, both private and government, for researching crime statistics and sex offender data. Don't forget that if you can find it, your prospective tenants can find it as well, and they will.

Local police departments are also a resource for crime stats, but online research can provide faster results and comparisons of areas. One example is doing home searches on CLRSearch.com. For example, we searched on two zip codes in Memphis, TN and went to the crime statistics for each.

In the charts below, you'll see the crime in a zip code compared to a national average set at 100. The crime rate in that zip code and for the state of TN will both be compared. A number higher than 100 indicates a higher crime rate than the national average, and lower indicates the opposite.

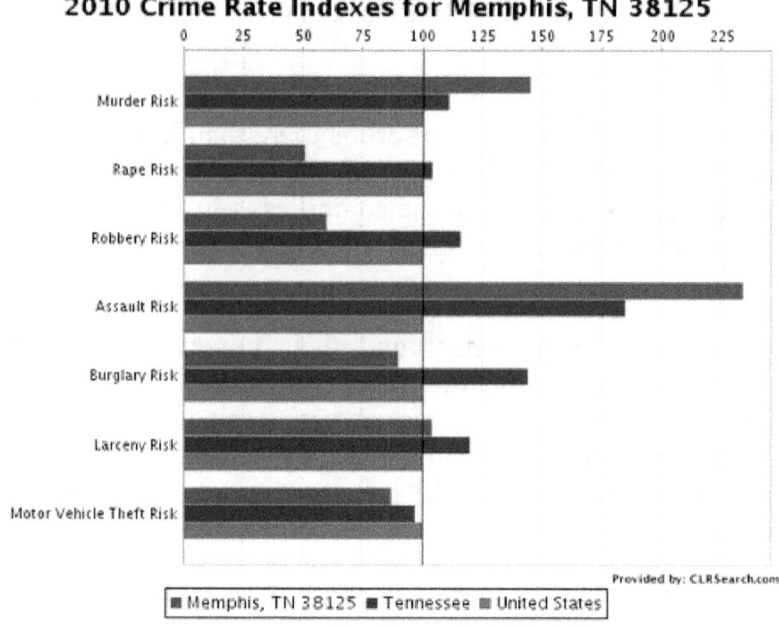

2010 Crime Rate Indexes	Memphis, TN 38125	Tennessee	United States
Total Crime Risk	97	133	100
Murder Risk	145	111	100
Rape Risk	51	104	100
Robbery Risk	60	116	100
Assault Risk	234	185	100
Burglary Risk	90	144	100
Larceny Risk	104	120	100
Motor Vehicle Theft Risk	87	97	100

In the 38125 zip code we see that the crime rate is lower than the U.S. average for Total Crime Risk, while the state has a third higher risk of crime than the national average.

Now, let's look at zip code 38127 to see the numbers for another area in which we have possible investment opportunities:

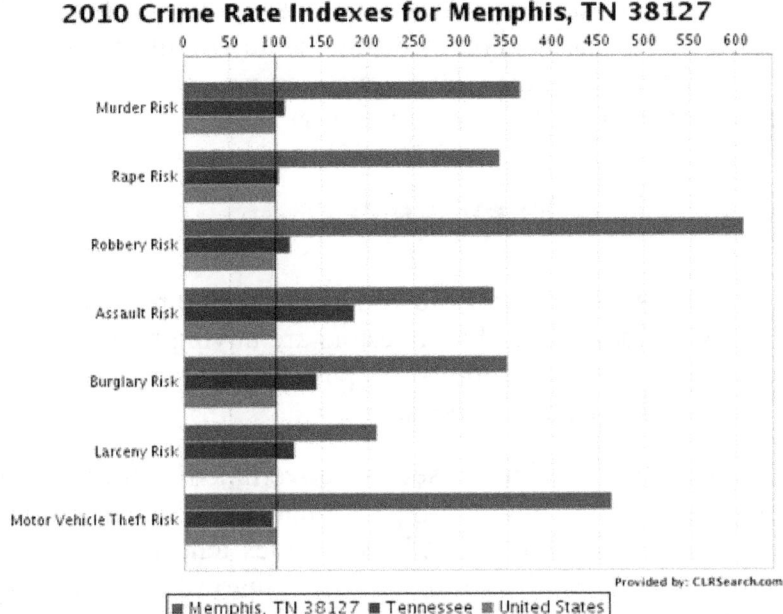

2010 Crime Rate Indexes for Memphis, TN 38127

2010 Crime Rate Indexes	Memphis, TN 38127	Tennessee	United States
Total Crime Risk	394	133	100
Murder Risk	366	111	100
Rape Risk	343	104	100
Robbery Risk	608	116	100
Assault Risk	336	185	100
Burglary Risk	351	144	100
Larceny Risk	209	120	100
Motor Vehicle Theft Risk	464	97	100

There's quite a different picture here, even though these areas aren't that far apart in location. The overall Total Crime Risk is almost four times the national average and three times the state average.

The blue-chip real estate investor will target areas with below-average crime rates. Not only will these areas command higher rents, they'll experience less turn-over, better cash flow, and higher resale values.

Beyond better tenant safety and lower vacancy rates, there's the property crime risk of the landlord. Losing one air conditioner outdoor unit can cost $1500 or more. That much money can dramatically impact the investment return for an entire year.

Employment

You can't pay rent without a job, and you can't pay top rents without a good job with good pay. Blue-chip investors are buying properties that will attract tenants with the ability to pay higher rents for higher quality homes in better neighborhoods.

The quality and stability of businesses and government facilities in the area greatly impact the long term performance of rental property investments. Areas with colleges and universities tend to have pretty stable employment, as well as those with military and government facilities. Large established corporations, the same ones you'd consider for your retirement stock portfolio, normally maintain a stable presence.

Research the local employment picture, and pay attention to any government or taxation initiatives that could bring about a change. While a major employer's departure may not destroy an area, it can certainly change the tenant demographics, resulting in lower rents or turnover and higher vacancy rates. In times of high unemployment, as in the 9% average at the end of 2011, areas that have maintained their job base through tough times may be areas in which you may want to invest.

Amenities

Related to location, the amenities in an area are important to buyers and renters. The proximity of green areas and parks is important to many people, especially in urban areas. Entertainment and cultural options, theaters, golf courses, and museums all influence choices of where to buy or rent.

As more older areas in cities are rejuvenated and factories or commercial buildings convert to lofts, restaurants and clubs, homes nearby can become more appealing in today's high gas cost environment. People want to spend more entertainment time closer to home.

Development, Permits, Comings & Goings

Time doesn't stand still, nor does the makeup of an area. That is, unless it's a designated historical district. Both commercial and residential areas are subject to zoning changes and changes in structure use. Homes become offices, and offices become lofts and condos. Factories become shopping malls.

In your research of an area, read the business news and pay attention to the initiatives and tax breaks from governments related to commercial enterprise. Sometimes allowing business into a previously residential-only neighborhood can be a problem. Other times, if it brings quaint shops and coffee shops, it can be a good thing for property values.

Listings and Vacancies

This is a good time to talk about "absorption rate." This is the rate at which properties listed for sale are being absorbed in the market area. When one compares the current absorption rate to an average over recent history, it's possible to draw some conclusions as to possible price movements.

If listings are going up and sales down, the absorption rate will go down, and properties stay on the market longer. This can have a depressing influence on resale prices. If the current number of listings is down and sales brisk, then properties are being absorbed faster, and fewer of them will be available … a positive influence on prices.

From the rental perspective, are there a large number of "for rent" advertisements for the area? This will directly impact rents and return on investment. Competition stiffens, and landlords lower rents or give other incentives to keep tenants.

Function

We covered functional obsolescence a bit previously. The function and appeal of a property has a limited shelf life without significant expense for renovation. Purchasing penny properties is definitely one way to get trapped in an investment that becomes functionally obsolete.

Outdated design features and dysfunctional floor plans are very common, and they don't contribute to a long term profitable investment strategy. These functional problems are not easily corrected, and even if they are, it's very costly in most cases.

Higher quality tenants move toward more modern layouts and design. Those investors holding functionally obsolete properties will lose these quality tenants to blue-chip property investors. In looking at the surrounding neighborhood, does it really make sense to purchase a low-priced property at $50,000 that needs $20,000 in upgrades? It's doubtful, especially if the rest of the neighborhood isn't doing the same upgrading. Again, historic districts are exceptions, as owners there tend to invest in modernization.

Greer and Colby, in their *Investment Analysis for Real Estate Decisions* tell us:

"A property's physical characteristics – building and other site improvements – by their very nature have limited useful lives. As their usefulness wanes, the facility becomes less desirable relative to competing properties that are newer or have been better maintained. Diminished usefulness due to declining conformity with current standards leads inevitably to a decreasing share of marketwise rental

revenue. The loss of competitive position due to defective or dated design or engineering is called functional obsolescence."

It's not just a matter of lost rent over time, or vacancy rates. When it comes time to exit the investment, functional obsolescence can reduce the selling price and require a lot more market time to find a buyer, increasing holding costs.

It isn't easy to sell a functionally obsolescent home. There are investor stories to back that up. Always be thinking of exiting an investment even before you enter it. The overall performance of a rental property investment can be significantly reduced if your exit price is less than anticipated.

Age – The Maintenance Factor

We've already mentioned that the goal of the blue-chip investor is to purchase homes that are at an average age or newer. The average age of the U.S. housing stock is currently 32 years. So, as blue-chip investors, we are searching for homes that age or newer. The primary influence of age on cash flow is its reduction due to higher maintenance costs for older structures.

Operating a home includes costs for utilities, maintenance, property taxes and insurance. Utilities and maintenance will normally vary with the age of the home. Over time, building codes change, and many of those changes have been related to construction materials and energy efficiency.

Older homes will be less efficient, requiring more money for heating and cooling. Older homes will also carry higher maintenance and repair costs.

- aging climate equipment
- wear and tear in virtually every area of the structure
- plumbing and electrical repairs

The American Housing Survey, conducted in odd-numbered years by the U.S. Census Bureau, collects extensive data on each home in the survey, and includes detailed data on operating costs. The data supports the statement that, whether per square foot or per dollar of house value, operating costs tend to be lower for newer homes.

While the data tells us age changes operating cost, too many investors use the same maintenance factor to evaluate every home regardless of age. In reality, newer homes should be given a maintenance cost reduction advantage in the evaluation process.

Tenants actually aggravate the situation, as the annual turnover is 61% and the average tenant occupancy is three years. This is opposed to an average 7 year occupancy for homeowners.

Costs to operate a home, over and above maintenance and repair, also include utilities, fuels and insurance. Studies show that homes built before 1960 have an average total cost of operation of $1.54 per square foot in size. This slides in age brackets to $1.27 per square foot for homes built between 1990 and1995.

When calculating a home's maintenance cost for a blue-chip and newer property, adjust it downward. For example, a home built in 1960 may have a 17% maintenance factor, while one built in 1990 may require only 10%.

Median Priced Neighborhood Discount Buying

It may seem like a contradiction to go through nine chapters talking about "blue-chip" real estate properties then to advise that you buy in a median priced neighborhood. Why not in neighborhoods that carry higher price tags? "Blue-chip" isn't a price related term, though paying the right price is part of a quality investment. Relate blue-chip to overall quality of a rental property investment and more factors must be considered.

The primary reason for buying in a median priced neighborhood is that it's in those neighborhoods that the majority of average Americans live. This provides the largest number of potential tenants, and homes that they can afford to rent. More than that though, these are the owner-occupied neighborhoods. Areas heavily owner-occupied provide benefits that add to the quality of the investment:

- **Upkeep** – owners have a vested interest in maintaining and growing their property values, so they will keep their homes and the neighborhood in better condition and more appealing to potential buyers.
- **Stability** – we've mentioned average time in occupancy for renters versus owners, and owners stay in their homes longer, providing stability to the neighborhood and higher resale value than areas heavy with rentals.
- **Value** – areas heavy with investor-owned rental homes will always create a discounted resale environment where your 70%-80% of value purchase will sell at that same discount, while in an owner occupied neighborhood you may pay 70% to 90% of value, but you'll sell at 90% to 100%.

It's a target you can hit!

This chapter is all about targeting the right blue-chip property, and it may seem like the ten different factors we discussed would make it very difficult to zero in on your target. While there are homes that are "perfect," meeting all ten of these requirements, your goal is to do a thorough analysis, weigh the results and data, and make a decision. You may trade off in one criteria for an outstanding fit in another, but the end result will be a blue-chip property.

Chapter 10

The Property Location & Selection Process

Success, and especially repetitive success, in real estate investment requires a process that's thorough, has been tested and proved successful, and the investor has the ability to replicate the process over and over. When a flaw is eradicated or a barrier overcome, the problem and solution are recorded and become a part of the future process.

Games of chance have a certain glamour, and humans like a bit of risk … in their games. However, risk in investments is to be avoided or minimized. The reward in relation to the risk should be substantial. The process we'll be moving through here is one that minimizes risk by thoroughly analyzing the variables and applying previously successful models to make the right decisions. It's a blue-chip strategy that will result in blue-chip returns with reduced risk.

Our Target Property

Æ3 bed / 2 bath minimum

Æ2 car storage

ÆMedian-priced neighborhoods

Æ1978 or newer

ÆGood schools

ÆLow crime

ÆOwner-occupied neighborhoods

This is to refresh your memory from previous chapters. These are the characteristics that result in excellent ROI with low risk, our blue-chip goal.

For our example investment, in the next chapter we'll look at neighborhoods and properties in the Memphis, TN Metro area. We'll clearly illustrate the comfort level that's attained when an investment has met the criteria for blue-chip status. Right now, let's look at the process of locating and evaluating properties.

Our Property Location Process

Scan universe of 10,000+ listings		
Pull data from public & private listings	Verify basic information, load into database	Price, zip code, age/condition, size, etc.

Due diligence on 750+ listings			
Investor objective parameters	Visual validation	Rent income & neighborhood analysis	Reduce to actionable list

Potential inventory of 100+ properties for potential investment				
Property Analysis	Cash flow projection	Inspection & renovation	Photos and video	Investable product

Locating Properties – Internet Searching

Unlike searching for properties 10 years ago, having to contact a real estate agent with a book or proprietary database, now there is almost unlimited access on the Internet to all properties listed for sale. Let's look at some of the resources, and their strengths and weaknesses.

Realtor.com

Originally owned outright and totally controlled by the National Association of Realtors® (NAR), Realtor.com is now a separate entity owned by Move.com and still holding exclusive deals with NAR for Web display of all listings of participating Realtor members.

When local Realtor members place their listings in their local MLS, Multiple Listing Service, they are imported automatically into the Realtor.com system. However, all of the information in a local MLS listing isn't displayed at Realtor.com, and some of it is manipulated in order to conform to the site's requirements.

While being a member of NAR and able to use the Realtor trademark used to mean that your listings would certainly be included at Realtor.com, some individual companies and regional groups have chosen to remove their listings for various reasons. So, Realtor.com no longer includes all of the member listings, which is the vast majority of listings in the country.

While this site may still hold the title for the most "listings," they're not all there, and you aren't normally searching the entire United States anyway. You're interested in a particular area, and you can go much closer to the source and get the same updated information from the local Realtors, and more of it.

IDX, Internet Data Exchange

 If you do searches for the local area and the term "real estate," as in *Memphis TN real estate*, you'll turn up a number of top results

that are local real estate brokerages. Most of them are cooperating in the local MLS, and they are using the IDX, Internet Data Exchange agreement for NAR members. An IDX logo or rendition of it will be on their search page in most cases. This is where Realtor.com gets their information, so you've moved to the source.

However, there is normally a lot more information available with each listing, and it hasn't been modified to fit another site's formatting or requirements. It's just as the listing broker/agent entered it. That requires another statement you'll find somewhere that is the disclaimer of accuracy. It's entered by people, so there are going to be errors. Never rely solely on what's in the listing information.

As the members all agree to only display certain information, you should find all of the same listings with the same data fields on any local participant's site. However, some will have paid to have a better interface for the site visitor, so try a few sites to see which works best for you.

Many people, and unfortunately some real estate agents, are not aware that most current MLS databases allow the member agent to create custom searches for their visitors that will allow the visitor to enter their property criteria and have automated email alerts sent to them when new properties come on the MLS that match. Price changes or other major edits that change listings that match the criteria will also arrive via email.

Some sites allow the visitor to do this themselves, while with many you'll have to contact the agent and give them your criteria so they can create the search for you. Savvy Web marketers will have a form right on the search page to get your information.

This alert system will keep you on top of the market daily with updates about properties that match your selection criteria. You can watch properties for price reductions and other status changes that could move them up on your consideration list.

Trulia, Zillow, and Other Sites

There are a number of other large sites that aggregate listings, including For Sale By Owner listings that you will not find on Realtor.com or local Realtor sites. Two of the largest are Zillow.com and Trulia.com.

These two sites do not receive automated feeds of local MLS listings, so will not have all of them. They do have local real estate companies posting their listings manually. They also use local government data about sales and tax assessor data to supplement the information they display. You can get sold property data and even estimates of value.

It's good to use one or both of these sites in conjunction with a local Realtor's IDX search, as there is extra information of value. Don't over-rely on value estimates though, as they can be less than accurate. Also, a big complaint at the time this was written is that these sites have no way for listings to be automatically removed when sold. Many real estate agents are not going in and removing listings when they come off the market, meaning that you'll have to check another source to be sure a home is still for sale.

Due Diligence & Property Selection

Once you have your search process lined out, you'll need to narrow down the many choices that will be presented. You're likely to get listings almost daily that seem to meet at least in part your blue-chip property criteria.

Neighborhoods for Blue-Chip Properties

Hopefully, you first did some neighborhood analysis, and you have selected target neighborhoods with the blue-chip characteristics we've discussed. Then you can have your Web searches restricted to those neighborhoods, allowing you to only be researching properties likely to meet your requirements.

Find the neighborhoods that have homes in the median price range most affordable to the greatest number of renters. You can set your price range search a little above and a little below. You will not likely be paying list price, so searching a few thousand over could provide a good candidate, or at least allow you to watch a home and wait for price reductions. Searching a little below could turn up a bargain that's already had the price reduced recently.

Neighborhood Rent Income Analysis

Part of your neighborhood targeting will be based on the rental market in that area. Are there many rental homes, or few? Are the mostly occupied, or mostly vacant? Call and research ads to get the average rents in the area for homes that most closely match our blue-chip property fundamentals and characteristics. Run some example number situations based on the rents you expect to be able to charge and the median price you'll be paying.

Characteristics

Set your search requirements to reflect the property characteristics we've discussed, bedrooms, baths, garage, etc. Your time is valuable, and you want to spend as much of it as possible in evaluating the very best investment candidates. By setting your searches up for only those, you'll be focusing on the very best for your due diligence.

Drive By and Look

There's no substitute for a first-hand view of a home, the street it's on, and the neighborhood. Real estate agents try to use photos and words to enhance a property in their marketing, so you'll want to actually drive around the neighborhood and drive by the homes that are at the top of your list of prospects.

The Premium List & Final Cut

Using the searches, example number-crunching and at least an exterior look at the homes on your short list, you'll be trying to narrow the field to the top few properties. Part of this process is asking for documents to examine, such as:

- property condition disclosures
- zoning & survey or plat
- subdivision, homeowner or condominium documents, covenants and restrictions
- previous appraisal if available, with a drawing & square footage calculation
- county tax records

Those subdivision or condominium covenants and restrictions are critical. You may find restrictions on long term rental of homes in some areas. It's not common, but would be a severe blow if you buy then get a letter from the association telling you to cease renting the home.

You'll also want to place any vehicle, parking or other restrictions that apply into your lease, so your tenants will abide by the rules. Far from a negative, one of the characteristics of a blue-chip rental property is a well-kept neighborhood and all of the residents abiding by the rules in order to keep it that way.

Your Property Walk-Through & Inspection

Once you've narrowed your choices to the best, you'll want to schedule visits and carefully examine each property personally or have your property manager or real estate investment company representative walk through the property for you. Whomever is scheduling these visits for you, a real estate agent or other party, be sure that you tell them that you'll be thorough, and that you'll take photos, and maybe even video. You want them to schedule enough time.

This is a critical part of your selection process, and you'll want to make notes, maybe with a voice recorder, as well as take photos and even video of the street, exterior on all sides, and many interior shots.

You'll not be making an immediate decision, and you'll want to be able to remember important things when comparing several properties later.

Much more than just a walk-through, you or someone representing you will be looking for any deferred maintenance issues and items that will require repair or cosmetic work before you install a tenant. Make sure that you note these and take photos, as you can use this information later to estimate costs. Your overall impression of how well the home has been maintained will be important, especially after you've gained experience.

Combine Information & Do Your CMA

We went over the Comparative Market Analysis process in an earlier chapter, and you can get your real estate agent to do one as well if you are using an agent. Once you have your two CMAs done, the one based on past sales and the one comparing current listings and competition, you'll have a good value estimation.

Using the price you want to pay, you can run the numbers for investment return on the short list of properties. This should bring you to a decision and the property on which you want to make an offer. In Chapter 12 we'll get into the negotiation and contract-to-closing process. First, let's look at some real-life investment scenarios.

Outsourcing the Process

We've all heard of outsourcing, normally as a cost-saving measure for companies to get specialized work done by experts without putting them on the payroll. That's not quite what we're talking about here, but close.

There are companies that specialize in packaging real estate investments, including managing the property if that's a requirement as well.

The Property Location Process

These real estate investment companies specialize in locating investment grade real estate properties. For residential rentals, they would scour the market area on a continuous basis, locating potential investment properties and evaluating them for investment quality.

These companies are staffed to take over the work many individual investors can't do, or they don't have the time to adequately canvas the market, missing properties because they don't have an effective process in place.

Evaluation and Valuation

These real estate investment companies then take each property apart to determine its condition, suitability for rental, neighborhood aesthetics, and overall appeal in the rental market. They do inspections and assess the condition of each property to determine when and how much might be required during the investment life in expenses for repairs and renovation.

Then a thorough financial analysis is done. First, a careful market analysis is completed that indicates the probable price that will have to be paid for the property. Following that analysis, another is done to understand the rental market, demographics and demand for this type and size of home as well as the neighborhood. A probable rental income is computed. Once these factors are uncovered and numbers computed, an investment return can be estimated with accuracy and a decision made as to the property's suitability for one or more of the investment company's clients.

Those properties deemed suitable are presented to selected clients who are able to make their investment with the assurance that all due diligence has been completed and that this will be a performing investment with a reasonably secure income outlook.

Where Do You Find These Companies?

There are a number of ways to uncover opportunities to invest with these turn-key real estate investment companies.

Web Search - Of course, there's always the Internet search. You'll turn up many companies, and will likely find one or more in your area. Carefully research their website and meet with them to learn how they conduct business and the experience of their personnel and contractors. More on that in a moment.

Other Investors – Your acquaintances with other investors is a good way to get recommendations for real estate investment companies like these. Particularly those investors you know are highly successful are great resources. Most will be willing to advise, even though there could be competitive situations as a result.

Real Estate Investment Clubs – Local real estate investment clubs are a great resource. You can ask other successful investors about these companies. However, you'll likely not need to do that, as they'll be members or affiliate members of the club, there to get business. They'll want to talk to you.

When It's a Remote Investment

These real estate investment companies bring value to the table, but it's even more pronounced when your business spreads outside of your local area. Investing in properties you can't see in a drive-by every week carries more risk. Some of that risk is the investor's lack of knowledge of the area and neighborhoods where they're investing.

Real estate investment companies can take away that area risk, as well as bring along their contacts, contractors and local legal and management resources necessary to acquire the most suitable rental properties and manage them for ongoing profits.

Buyer Beware – Do Your Due Diligence

A cautionary note is in order here. You'll have choices as to companies that provide these properties and services. You'll want to exercise great care in researching their reputations and expertise. The best way to illustrate the issues you'll encounter in making the wrong decision is with a real-life account from a contractor friend of mine. Here's his account of one investor's tribulations:

This is a tale of renovation headaches and profit destruction in using the wrong real estate investment company. Especially in renovation work, there must be a reliance on the quality of not only the real estate investment company, but also their selections of contractors and personnel.

I like to compare it to doing your own contracting in the renovation of your personal home. If you don't have experience in general contracting and the selection of sub-contractors, it's easy to end up choosing workers based on cost or bids. The lowest bid is usually in that position for a reason.

When you work with a real estate investment company, you must trust their ability to get a proper inspection done of the properties to uncover problems you don't want to discover later. Then, once the extent of the renovation is determined, their experience and standards in contractor selection make a huge difference in the outcome.

Our Investor Story

A gentleman who lived out of state called us in to try to help in extricating them from a deteriorating investment situation. He had purchased a property from a local investment company. They had advertised their "one stop shop" handling of investments, including an in-house team to do repairs and renovations.

This investor trusted the investment company, though they minimized the need for property inspections. They touted their experience and contractor expertise. Though things seemed to be going well at first, it didn't take long for problems to surface when the investor began to receive numerous and frequent "maintenance" invoices.

The maintenance bills kept coming, costs mounted, then the property went vacant. No tenant is going to suffer constant problems for very long. The investor decided to get involved at this point, and called in a third party for an independent property inspection.

This inspection turned up major problems, including a roof at the end of its useful life. There were also damaged rafters, and smoke damage eventually revealed a fire before the property was purchased and renovated. This situation probably was the reason the property was purchased at such a low price initially.

The list of problems has grown, and the home still isn't occupied by a tenant. The owner is contemplating legal action against the real estate investment company, another expensive proposition.

From my contractor friend's account, it's clear that all real estate investment companies aren't equal. An error in selection can destroy the return on investment in a property.

Chapter 11

Some Real Numbers
& A Tale of Two Properties

There's nothing like real-life examples to illustrate and validate a process, and blue-chip real estate investing has a wealth of information and many success examples. In this chapter, we'll first take you through a detailed analysis of the numbers for a successful blue chip investment in Memphis, TN.

You'll see the detail that goes into risk reduction and profit maximization in blue-chip investing. There is no stone left un-turned, as skipping steps leads to added risk and poor results.

Actual Blue-Chip Investment Breakdown

For this chapter's example investment property, we used our normal location process in Metro Memphis, TN. We studied the market, gathered information on neighborhoods and median prices, then zeroed in on a property.

We'll follow part of that process and do a thorough breakdown of the performance of the selected property over a 5 year holding period. This is the blue-chip investing process and results in action.

Discount Buy in High Quality Neighborhood

2012 YTD Home Sales (Memphis Metro) (Median Home Price)		
Collierville	$	280,000
Germantown	$	259,000
Lakeland	$	229,900
Arlington	$	192,083
Downtown	$	169,900
Southwind	$	168,000
Bartlett	$	150,000
Olive Branch	$	142,900
Cordova	$	108,000
Southaven	$	121,900
E. Memphis	$	106,000
Millington	$	89,767
Shelby County	$	82,500
Midtown	$	65,000
Hickory Hill	$	64,000
Raleigh / Cov Pike	$	49,000
Whitehaven	$	35,000
Parkway Village	$	32,000
Berclair / Highland Heights	$	24,000
Frayser	$	20,000
S. Memphis	$	11,500

Blue-chip Neighborhoods

The chart shows a really wide range of median neighborhood prices. We'll be shopping for a property at a median price of around $100,000. Note that the "blue-chip" neighborhoods, prior to any further investigation, are those in the shaded area of the chart. We've located a property that meets all of our requirements, and we've done all of the due diligence described in previous chapters. Now let's look at the details.

Example Property

- 3 bedroom
- 2 bath
- 2 car garage
- 1575 square feet
- 1990 construction
- SE Memphis location
- near FedEx World HQ & other jobs

- bank REO source
- cosmetic repairs
- like new renovation
- sold in 21 days
- rented in 4 days
- rent $1150/2 yr lease
- appraised $115,000
- sale price of $98,900

- Higher than U.S. average education and income in this neighborhood + primarily owner-occupied
- 14% discount from current market value
- 2 year lease to FedEx manager transferring into the area
- Planned 5 year hold with realistic exit of 9% increase over current market value

- $25,280 investment can provide secured 10% Return on Capital during hold + carry from sale

Permanent Loan

Loan Amount ($79,120)
Cash due at close ($25,280)
Monthly payment ($442)

Cash Flow

Monthly cash flow (Y1) $217
Monthly cash flow (Y2) $217
Total profit (rent) $13,001
Total profit (sale) $17,212
Total profit 4 year hold $30,213

Profitability Metrics

Purchase cap rate 7.99%
Property discount 9%
Equity at close $35,880
Investment IRR 19.53%
Break Even (time) Year 5
Gross Rent Multiplier (annual) 7.17
Payback Ratio 3.2

	Year	Year	Year	Year	Year 5
Cash on cash return	10.29%	10.29%	10.29%	10.29%	178.37%
Debt coverage ratio	1.49	1.49	1.49	1.49	1.49
Operating expense ratio	36%	36%	36%	36%	36%
Break even ratio	71%	71%	71%	71%	71%
Interest carry ratio	9.99%	9.99%	9.99%	9.99%	9.99%

Cap rate	7.99%	6.87%	6.87%	6.87%	6.87%
Profit margin	21%	21%	21%	21%	**363%**

This is the real deal, and you should be getting excited about the logic of blue-chip investing. With lower risk, amazing returns are possible. It isn't done with cheap properties, but you don't have to trade off return for higher quality homes.

However, if you're still wondering about those lower-priced homes and if there's a better opportunity there, check out this tale of two properties.

Tale of Two Properties

The contrast in investment results between a blue-chip property and one that seems like a good investment on the surface can be quite educational. Let's take a look at a real-world comparison of two properties.

Property A (Blue-chip)   Property B

These two properties were evaluated using the blue-chip strategy, and the attributes were compared. The next chart shows the results. A few notes:

*Annual vacancy includes the time the property is being readied, marketed and tenanted. Vacancy suggested on the blue-chip property,

Property A, is 1 month at 8% annual. This number seems conservative, but is based on the low number of vacant homes in the neighborhood and the rate of population growth. Vacancy on Property B is suggested at 16%. Property B's neighborhood has a rate of 400% of average U.S. crime, 750% more vacant homes than the blue-chip property's neighborhood, and the population is in decline.

** Ongoing maintenance was calculated using cost per square foot data from the U.S. Census Bureau, and based on the age of the homes.

*** Tenant turnover was calculated from U.S. average tenant turnover rates based on average home size and adjusted accordingly for each property.

****We are using a 4.75% interest rate for each property as quoted on 8/15/2011, though a potential penalty exists for the small loan size with Property B.

A Tale of Two Properties		
	Blue-chip	**Property B**
Price	$119,900	$50,000
Quality of Life		
Zip	38125	38127
Crime Index	97	394
Poverty	2.80%	25.90%
College Grads	29.74%	6.09%
Median Rent	$1,166	$636
Population change since 2000	57%	-16.00%
Population projection for 2014	19.54%	-11.16%
Long term outlook	Positive	Negative
Housing Stock		
Number of housing units	14,288	15,554
Renter Occupied	10.49%	32.80%
# of vacant homes for rent	57	432
1980 or newer homes	95.81%	15.16%
Purchase Scenario		
Price	$119,900	$50,000
Square footage	1780	1550
Rent	$1300	$685
Taxes	$122	$95
Insurance	$62	$42

Property management at 10%	$130	$68.50
Vacancy*	$104	$109.60
Ongoing maintenance**	$22.25	$32.25
Tenant turnover***	$103	$88.00
Principal & Interest****	$500.36	$208.66
Monthly Net	$256.39	$40.99
Annual	$3,076.68	$498.88
20% Down payment + closing	$28,480	$15,500
Annual ROI (Financed)	**10.80%**	**3.39%**
Annual ROI (Cash Purchase)	**7.51%**	**2.48%**

The blue-chip property neighborhood characteristics:

- average crime
- less than 3% of residents live in poverty
- nearly 30% of residents have college degrees
- the population is rapidly growing
- projected to grow another 20% between 2010 & 2014
- heavily owner occupied
- only 57 rental homes vacant
- 96% of homes newer than the 1980 U.S. average

Let's contrast the characteristics of Property B:

- 400% of the U.S. average crime rate
- more than 25% of population lives in poverty
- only 6% have finished college
- 432 vacant rental homes (750% than the blue-chip neighborhood)
- only 15% of homes are newer than average
- population is falling
- neighborhood is in decline

The facts, figures and demographics bear out that the blue-chip property will not only outperform Property B as an investment, it will increase more in value, resell easier and faster, and will have a greater life-expectancy.

The Differences are Clear – Invest in Blue-Chip Properties

You know what to look for, how to value it, where to buy, and how much of a difference going "blue-chip" can make. Let's get into doing a deal.

Chapter 12

The Negotiation & Contract to Closing

While there's a period of relaxation of tensions once a purchase contract and price are agreed upon, a real estate transaction is really a continuing negotiation all the way through the closing. There are various points at which one party is requiring something of the other, and this results in either agreement or a counter proposal, but still a negotiation.

It almost resembles a team sporting event, with the buyer and seller each having support members helping them to handle their side of the negotiation and transaction. However, there does not have to be a clear winner and loser, as there is no scoring. In fact, the more it resembles a rough-and-tumble sporting event, the less satisfying it will be for all concerned and the greater the risk of a deal that doesn't make it to closing.

As an investor, you'll become quite comfortable with the many variables involved in a real estate transaction, and you're in love with the numbers, not the house anyway. However, in many cases you'll be dealing with a normal homeowner with greater emotion involved in the transaction. And, if this is a distress situation, such as a short sale or pre-foreclosure, there will be even more stress on the other side of the deal.

The First Offer & Earnest Money

One of the most common questions asked of real estate agents by buyers is the amount of their first offer on a home. The seller wants the most they can get of course, and the buyer wants to pay as little as possible. Most people, even real estate investors, want to strike a good deal but not reach the point of making an insulting offer.

What's an insulting offer? If it's a foreclosure owned by the bank, there's no such thing. You can get into flat rejection territory if you low-ball too aggressively. In general though, banks and lenders holding foreclosure homes are all business, so a low offer will generally just bring about a counter offer.

A bit more care should be taken when you're offering to purchase from a regular homeowner, particularly when they're not in distress. The same goes for a real estate investment company that may have already purchased the foreclosure, renovated the property, and place a tenant for you. This is often the case with blue-chip properties. They're homes that have been well cared for by a homeowner who values the property. Too low of an initial offer can result in no second chance if they're insulted.

Or, a low offer may not send you packing, but get you a counter offer that will end up costing you dearly. An actual example is a buyer offering to purchase a lakefront property, a small house with a young couple who had received parental help in getting the home. This buyer is an investor wanting to use the property as a vacation rental, and it would be an excellent investment for this purpose. Looking on it as a business deal, and against the advice of his real estate agent, the investor made a low-ball offer.

The good news is that the sellers didn't send him packing, but the counter offer was FIRM, and one dollar OVER full asking price. Basically, the sellers were offended, but their agent advised them to counter at or near full price to pull up the buyer's offer. They added the dollar as a statement. And, that's what the buyer ended up paying.

If you're dealing with a homeowner in distress, perhaps trying to work out a short sale offer with the lender, you're limited by the balance due on the mortgage and you'll be submitting the offer to the bank prior to foreclosure. Some lenders have eased and streamlined their short sales procedures to avoid the hassle and expense of a foreclosure, but the majority of short sale offers never make it to closing.

There are blue-chip properties that end up short sale possibilities. The owners have taken excellent care of the home, but they have fallen on hard times and want to avoid foreclosure. In this chapter we'll look at the short sale process in more detail, as it requires more involvement on the part of the buyer and the seller in structuring the offer to the bank.

Earnest Money

The amount of earnest money that accompanies an offer varies by region and custom. It's also very much up to the seller and their situation. While a $200,000 home purchase in one area may call for an earnest money deposit of $5000, in another it could be as little as $1000 or even less in distress situations.

Normally the real estate agent involved will be able to recommend the best earnest money to be offered. Sometimes it's even specified in the listing in some areas. If not, and your earnest money offer is low and there is interest in the property, the seller may come back and ask for more in their counter offer.

The Foreclosure Process

Generally, the better blue-chip opportunities don't come from foreclosure inventories. This is primarily due to the damage and disrepair issues associated with foreclosure properties. They've been empty for months, sometimes longer. And, because the process has stretched to almost a year on average, the homeowners may have stayed in the home, but they stopped taking care of it long before they had to move.

However, some banks and lenders are making efforts to spruce up properties, which wasn't their normal procedure in the past. Also, there are instances where people are offered "cash for keys." The bank pays them money to leave the home in good condition and just turn in their keys. It usually saves the lender some money, and the home could be in pretty good condition.

Another problem with foreclosures is that they tend to clump together, with too many in the same neighborhood. This reduces property values and the overall condition and salability of the neighborhood.

We have stressed the importance of neighborhood research and selection in blue-chip investing. However, sometimes there are instances of nice homes in great neighborhoods whose owners fell into financial trouble. If they're the exception rather than the rule, then there could be blue-chip potential.

So, it's possible that you'll locate a foreclosure home that is a blue-chip investment candidate. If so, we can take a look at the foreclosure offer through closing process first, as it's simpler than most others. Why?

- The bank will normally sell only "as is" without repair negotiations.
- The lender will not normally give any guarantees of title, though you can normally get title insurance.
- Either the bank will require cash or very secure financing, and it will be a shortened timeframe to closing.

Because the bank doesn't intend to pay for any repairs doesn't mean that you aren't going to do the inspections necessary to give you a clear picture of the condition of the property. You just normally will not be able to get the lender to take care of issues you turn up in your inspections. They are more for a "make or break" the deal decision.

The Short Sale Process

While banks gradually became easier to deal with in 2010 and 2011 when it came to short sale offers, they're far from a push-over. Many short sales never make it to closing due to the banks' refusal to approve the offers. If you're going to try to buy a home through a short sale, either work with a real estate agent experienced in the process or learn the basics and understand that you'll have to help the homeowner to make it happen.

The Due Diligence

You're not offering to buy the home from the homeowner in a short sale. It's already been decided that it can't be sold for enough money to pay commissions and pay off the mortgage, thus the "short" sale. The bank is accepting an amount short of the payoff, so must be convinced that the best approach is to take less than the mortgage balance and avoid foreclosure.

Knowing the market and being able to submit data with your offer that verifies its validity is the only way you can succeed. A thorough CMA, Comparative Market Analysis, showing that other very similar homes are selling in the same price range is your first priority. You must be able to submit data that proves the home is unlikely to command a higher price than your offer in the current market.

That's the market and property analysis, but you'll also have to do a homeowner financial analysis in preparation for the next step, the hardship letter. Have the homeowner gather EVERY document, bill, past due notice, or default notice that they have on all of their assets and accounts. Every dollar they're paying out should be documented.

The Short Sale Package

The short sale package will contain three items:

1. The hardship letter.
2. The CMA information and full debt, income and cash outflow accounting.
3. The offer.

You should have allowed for this to be a drawn-out process, and you'll definitely be waiting for responses from the bank that seem like they're taking forever. Many short sales don't close simply because buyers give up and get tired of waiting. And, have copies of everything, because the lender will likely ask for the same documents over again.

The Negotiation

Let's move on to more normal type deals, when you're going to be negotiating with a regular homeowner who has taken care of their property and isn't necessarily in financial distress. The negotiation process comes after your neighborhood and property selection due diligence discussed in previous chapters.

You know this is a good investment if bad things don't turn up in inspections or the title search. You also know your top number, the price at which going any higher would kill your interest in it as an investment. And, you know what you'd like to pay to realize your cash flow and return on investment goals.

Price isn't the only factor in a home purchase negotiation. There are a number of contingencies that could be a part of a purchase agreement and offer.

- Possible assumption or owner financing (full or partial).
- Personal property that could remain and pass to you at closing (example: portable storage building or free-standing hot-tub).
- Date of occupancy (the seller may want more time or a faster closing).
- Visible and noticed issues you require corrected before closing (example: broken garage door and defective opener).
- Which title company handles the transaction can be a negotiated item.
- Fees to be paid and by whom.

Any of those items or others could end up as contingencies that you require to be satisfied as conditions of purchase. They become a part of the purchase agreement or addendums to it, and a part of the negotiation. The seller may not have included that storage building in their listing, but they may be OK with letting it stay.

The seller will normally not accept your first offer, and will make a counter offer. This counter should address the contingencies in your initial offer, either accepting, rejecting, or compromising on each. Once the price and all other contingencies are settled, buyer and seller sign and it's a deal.

Disclosures

Depending on the area or state laws, you may be seeing disclosure documents before or after a negotiated purchase contract. If you get some or all of them before your offer, it can help you to avoid wasting time, and it's common to at least have access to the property condition disclosure before an offer is made.

The instructions given to the homeowner include the caution that they should err on the side of over-disclosure, being very thorough and entering everything they know about the property condition. However, the human memory is a funny thing, and sometimes for whatever reason, everything isn't disclosed.

In a few states a disclosure isn't even required, but may be a voluntary item. In any case, it's an important document. The buyer is making decisions based on the content of the disclosure, and if it's not truthful or information is omitted, buyers can be damaged and may have legal recourse.

Read all of the information carefully, and particularly make note of items left unanswered. It's interesting how some people really don't want to lie, and they think that just not answering a question is a better approach. If it's important information left blank, a wise choice would be to request it prior to making an offer.

In some states, there are deadlines for delivery of disclosures as well as deadline dates for objections to what's in them. Failing to meet those dates could result in the buyer losing their right to dispute the items or get out of the deal with their earnest money.

The Title Binder

The seller, or the seller's agent, will immediately order a title search and title insurance binder from a title company. This is normally done very quickly, as other participants in the transaction, such as the surveyor, will want to have a copy of this binder before they do their job.

The title company executes a thorough search of the public records to locate all documents, filings, easements or liens related to the property. These can go as far back as original government patents or land grants. This title search and the documents found will be thoroughly examined by the title company before issuing the title insurance binder or commitment.

This commitment binds the title company to provide title insurance at closing, but it does so with two major sections that must be examined carefully by the buyer, their agent, and/or their attorney.

Requirements

The title binder is issued contingent upon a list of requirements to be met prior to or at closing. Most of these are normal and expected, but there can be surprises or special items requiring action to keep the deal moving.

- **Deed** – a valid deed conveying title is required to be provided by the seller(s) and signed at closing.
- **Mortgage payoff** – any existing mortgages on the property will be required to be paid off.
- **Payment of taxes** – any past due or current taxes due must be paid at closing.
- **Lien or encumbrance removal** – if liens are found, such as a mechanic's lien for work performed but not paid for, it must be paid at closing.
- **Municipal services payment** – fees such as trash removal, water and sewer must be paid up to closing date.
- **Quitclaim deed(s)** – every now and then, a divorce or other situation leaves it unclear whether someone such as a previous spouse may have some interest in the property. If this is the case, the title company will require a quitclaim deed from that person to state they are quitting any claim to the property.

There are many items that can show up in the Requirements section, most of which are normal and not anything to be concerned about. Here's an image of some of the 16 requirements on a residential deal. None of the requirements were of a nature that they couldn't be easily resolved prior to closing.

ALTA COMMITMENT FOR TITLE INSURANCE
SCHEDULE B
SECTION ONE
REQUIREMENTS

File Number: ████████   Commitment: ████████

The following are the requirements to be complied with:

1. Payment of the full consideration to, or for the account of, the grantors or mortgagors.

2. Payment of all taxes, charges, assessments, levied and assessed against subject premises, which are due and payable.

3. Satisfactory evidence should be had that improvements and/or repairs or alterations thereto are completed; that contractor, subcontractors, labor and materialmen are all paid.

4. Instruments(s) creating the estate or interest to be insured must be approved, executed and filed for record to wit:

5. **Provide this company with a currently dated Improvement Location Report on the subject property, if deletions are required by lender or purchaser.**

6. **Payment of the 2009 taxes, owner #74852, assessment #09-2744.**

7. **Any assessments related to the subject property including but not limited to garbage, homeowners associations, road maintenance for the year 2010 and previous.**

8. **Release of ████████ Mortgage, dated October 25, 2006 from ████████, as to a life Estate, ████████ ████████ and ████████, as to the remained interest subject to a condition subsequent; ████████,**

Exceptions

Exceptions to coverage is the other important section, as these are situations, circumstances and property peculiarities that will not be insured by the title insurance company. As with requirements, some of these are expected and normal. However, it's in exceptions that you want to be careful to fully understand everything you see and what this means to you as the buyer and new owner.

First, just because something or a situation is "excepted" from coverage, it isn't necessarily a risk factor you need to be concerned with. Title insurance companies routinely except from coverage all documents of record and what those documents contain. That's because these are public record documents that normally transfer with the land and can't be amended or disposed of. So, if the document or situation exists, you should be aware of it and accept it, as you will not be able to file a claim for relief, defense or reimbursement from your title insurer later in relation to these excepted items. Examples include:

- **Covenants & Restrictions** – in an earlier chapter, we discussed subdivision covenants and restrictions that run with the property and normally can't be changed without the agreement of at least a majority of the property owners via voting.
- These are recorded at the courthouse, and become an exception on the title binder. This means that if you buy the home with a restriction against any outdoor temporary storage buildings, you can't file a claim for relief from the title insurer because you can't install one. Whatever these documents say is what goes, and you can't claim damage later because of these rules.
- **Easements** – utilities frequently have easements along the edges of property lines for the installation and maintenance of electrical, gas, cable, and other utility conduits. If there is a ten foot utility easement along the edge of your property, it will be an exception, and you can't claim damage later because you installed a concrete patio into the easement and it is damaged by the utility company.
- **Deed restrictions** – a previous deed, even ten owners back, that "legally" precludes a certain use for the property will be excepted. Legally is important. A deed restriction that's not legal, such as limiting selling to a minority isn't enforceable. However, one that states that there can never be a business of any type on the property (even if legal zoning-wise) would be excepted and you can't claim damage because of it later.
- **Survey notations** – the surveyor will note anything they see at the property, including things like old downed fences, or even rough dirt roads entering or crossing the property. These items will be excepted because they exist and could indicate a possible claim by others. Whose downed fence is it, and why is it there? Who has been driving across the property, and could they claim the right to continue to do so?

There are some exceptions that may show up and kill a deal, as they are usually not correctable, and their discovery during this process may give a buyer second thoughts. An example would be an easement for a high voltage overhead line that hasn't been installed. If the utility company will not agree to remove the easement, or they can't, the buyer may decide to back out of the deal.

SECTION TWO
EXCEPTIONS

File Number: ▉▉▉▉▉▉▉   Commitment: ▉▉▉▉▉▉▉

Standard exceptions 1, 2, 3 4, 6 and /or 8 may be deleted from any policy, and standard exception 7 may be modified on any policy, upon compliance with all provisions of the applicable regulations, upon payment of all additional premiums required by the applicable regulations, upon receipt of the required documents and upon compliance with the company's underwriting standards for each such deletion. Standard exception 5 may be deleted from the policy if the named insured in the case of an owner's policy, or the vestee, in the case of a loan policy, is a corporation, a partnership, or other artificial entity, or a person holding title as trustee. The policy to be issued pursuant to this commitment will be endorsed or modified in schedule B by the company to waive its rights to demand arbitration pursuant to the conditions and stipulations of the policy at no cost or charge to the insured. The endorsement or the language added to Schedule B of the policy shall read: "In compliance with Subsection D of 13.14.18.10. NMAC, the company herby waives its rights to demand arbitration pursuant to the title insurance arbitration rules of the American Land Title Association. Nothing herein prohibits the arbitration of all arbitrable matters when agreed to by both company and the insured." 16-16-/9, 3-1-90, 6-1-97, 6-1-98; 13.14.5.9 NMAC – Rn, 13 NMAC 14.5.9,5-15-00;A, 8-29-06; A, 7-1-05

Schedule B of the policy or policies to be issued will contain exceptions to the following matters unless the same are disposed of to the satisfaction of the company.

1. Rights or claims of parties in possession not shown by the public records.

2. Easements, or claims of easements, not shown by the public records.

3. Encroachments, overlaps, conflicts in boundary lines, shortages in area, or other matters which would be disclosed by an accurate survey and inspection of the premises.

4. Any lien, claim or right to a lien, for services, labor or material heretofore or hereafter furnished, imposed by law and not shown by the public records.

5. Community property, survivorship, or homestead rights, if any, of any spouse of the insured (or vestee in a leasehold or loan policy).

The image is a partial copy of the exceptions section in a residential real estate title insurance binder. The important thing to remember about Exceptions is that you should carefully examine them and ask the questions you need to be sure that you understand them. Once the deal has closed, your insurance is only as promised or excepted in this binder and in your policy.

Inspections

The first due diligence item for the buyer is to commission property inspections right away. There will be due dates for the completion of the inspections, as well as deadline dates to object to deficiencies noted. Failure to object by the deadline dates can preclude the buyer from getting out of the deal with their earnest money intact if they can't come to agreement on inspection items.

PURCHASE AGREEMENT – RESIDENTIAL RESALE – 2010

Unless otherwise agreed in writing, the Buyer will select the inspector. Whether or not the transaction closes, the following inspections will be paid for by:

INSPECTIONS	Buyer Pays	Seller Pays	Delivery Deadline	Objection Deadline	Resolution Deadline
Home	XX		10 DAYS FR ACCEPTANCE	5 DAYS FROM DELIVERY	5 DAYS FR OBJECTION DELIVERY
Electrical	XX		10 DAYS FR ACCEPTANCE	5 DAYS FROM DELIVERY	5 DAYS FR OBJECTION DELIVERY
Heating/Air Conditioning	XX		10 DAYS FR ACCEPTANCE	5 DAYS FROM DELIVERY	5 DAYS FR OBJECTION DELIVERY
Plumbing	XX		10 DAYS FR ACCEPTANCE	5 DAYS FROM DELIVERY	5 DAYS FR OBJECTION DELIVERY
Roof	XX		10 DAYS FR ACCEPTANCE	5 DAYS FROM DELIVERY	5 DAYS FR OBJECTION DELIVERY
Structural	XX		10 DAYS FR ACCEPTANCE	5 DAYS FROM DELIVERY	5 DAYS FR OBJECTION DELIVERY
Lead-Based Paint Evaluation					
Risk Assessment					
Paint Inspection					
Combination Risk Assessment/Inspection					
Other:					
Well Equipment (pump, pressure tank, lines)	XX		10 DAYS FR ACCEPTANCE	5 DAYS FROM DELIVERY	5 DAYS FR OBJECTION DELIVERY
Well Water Potability Tests	XX		10 DAYS FR ACCEPTANCE	5 DAYS FROM DELIVERY	5 DAYS FR OBJECTION DELIVERY
Well Water Yield Tests	XX		10 DAYS FR ACCEPTANCE	5 DAYS FROM DELIVERY	5 DAYS FR OBJECTION DELIVERY
Well Water Nitrate Tests					
Pool/Spa/Hot Tub Equipment			10 DAYS FR ACCEPTANCE	5 DAYS FROM DELIVERY	5 DAYS FR OBJECTION DELIVERY
Wood-Destroying Insects	XX		10 DAYS FR ACCEPTANCE	5 DAYS FROM DELIVERY	5 DAYS FR OBJECTION DELIVERY
Dry Rot	XX		10 DAYS FR ACCEPTANCE	5 DAYS FROM DELIVERY	5 DAYS FR OBJECTION DELIVERY
Radon	XX		10 DAYS FR ACCEPTANCE	5 DAYS FROM DELIVERY	5 DAYS FR OBJECTION DELIVERY
Mold	XX		10 DAYS FROM ACCEPTANCE	5 DAYS FROM DELIVERY	5 DAYS FROM OBJECTIONS DELIVERY
Square-Foot Measurement:					
Sewer Line Inspections					

The image is a sample of a purchase contract section with the inspections outlined with due dates. The format varies significantly by state, but the important points are that the inspections should be performed and objections/correction negotiations completed within contract deadlines. In this case, hard dates aren't used to provide flexibility, but "10 days after delivery" becomes a hard date when delivery is made.

Repair Negotiations

With the blue-chip investment process, there should be fewer problems with condition and repair disputes that kill deals. That's because the blue-chip investor is selecting properties in excellent condition and well-maintained by their owners. However, there can be things turned up in inspections that require negotiation and correction.

Cash buyers have more latitude in most cases in negotiating repairs or accepting the home as-is and fixing things themselves. When a lender is involved, they may examine the inspection reports and require certain repairs to be made before closing and final loan approval.

Example: The general inspector finds a leak the homeowner had never noticed in one bathroom that has compromised some of the materials in the floor under and around the bathtub. It's estimated to be in the neighborhood of a $1500 repair. Some of the possible outcomes include:

- It's a cash deal, the buyer has made a good purchase, and decides to buy it as-is and do the repair.
- Cash or financed, the buyer could ask for a $1500 credit to the selling price and make the repair after closing. If the lender balks, then instead of a credit, the lender may allow the $1500 to be placed in escrow and the repair done after closing.
- The lender or the buyer wants the repair done before closing. The seller brings in the repair people and has the work done and re-inspected by the buyer's original inspector.
- The seller refuses to make the repair, cut the price, or escrow the money. The buyer can then decide whether to proceed to closing or back out of the deal.

In normal buyer/seller transactions, inspections and repairs are the most common deal-killers. Some buyers are surprised by how stubborn a seller can be about paying for repairs. This is even though the buyer had them over a price barrel and has cut their cash coming out of the deal to the point that they can't afford the repairs. It's a balance, and sometimes if the buyer has really made an amazing price deal they may have to accept making the repairs.

Appraisal

Even in a cash deal, a buyer can require an appraisal if they so desire. However, it's definitely going to happen when there is going to be a mortgage. Even though the buyer is probably paying for this appraisal, it's ordered by the lender. The appraiser is working for and chosen by the lender.

Since the housing and mortgage problems that began in 2007, stricter rules were adopted for appraisals, and procedures were changed supposedly making it harder to submit inflated appraisals. There have been many complaints that the new procedures and rules have mostly just managed to kill deals, as appraisers brought in from other areas may not know the value of homes elsewhere.

Lenders have become much more cautious as well, and they are being strict with their appraisers and placing more liability on them in case of errors. So, appraisals can err on the side of conservatism and avoiding liability. This can kill deals when the homes don't appraise to the selling price.

Review appraisals are also becoming more common. A second appraiser is called in to review the work done by the first. Lenders are being super cautious. Pretty much, the buyer is paying but doesn't really have a lot of input into this process. While a buyer can request another appraisal if the first one falls short, the lender may not accept it, and it will add to the cost.

Should the appraisal come up short, there is normally language in the purchase contract for the situation. The seller can reduce their price to the appraised value. Or, the buyer can put more money into the deal to bring the equity to the 20% or so minimum required by the lender. There could be a combination of both of those approaches. The final option is the collapse of the deal.

Great Deal – But Only So-so Appraisal?

As investors, we're crunching the numbers and working toward the very best deal with the highest return on investment. And, if we do things right, we'll be buying blue-chip properties at below their current market value. This locks in equity from the first day, a profit when we take possession.

So, we should see that equity in the appraisal … right? Nope, not often. Even before the troubles beginning in 2007, it was quite common for the appraisal amount to come in at precisely the selling price. When it did come in above, it was only a small percentage. That's the situation now, only more so.

It's a conservative financial world today with mortgages. There is really no incentive for an appraiser to come in with a value over the selling price. They work for the lender, and the lender only needs to see the selling price for the appraised value to make the deal happen. Appraising higher than that only adds risk to the appraiser if the buyer defaults later and the lender looks to the appraiser to justify their number.

So, expect an appraisal at the selling price, or only slightly higher, no matter what you know the true market value to be. If you really want to see this is true, just go in for a refinance a few months later and ask for the true value. You'll probably get it, as there's a new set of data and no selling price as a target appraisal result.

The Mortgage Process & Funding

The appraisal is part of the mortgage process, but the lender is examining many of the other documents as well. They're also doing further checks on the borrower's credit and financial situation, many times right up to the day of closing.

In many cases, closing dates are not met, and it's due to the lender's failure to do final approval and release funds. Their increased caution over the last few years means that some documents are examined over and over, re-requested, and examined again. Since some of these documents come from appraisers, surveyors, inspectors and others, any small delays on their part are amplified in the mortgage process.

Get the Keys

Once all of the pieces of the closing puzzle are in place, you can come to the closing table with your money, your lender will fund the deal, and you can leave with the keys. Normally you will have done a walk-through one or two days prior, or maybe even as late as the morning of the closing. If you live outside the area, have your agent, property manager, or real estate investment company get you photos of a final walk through on your behalf.

Your walk-through is for the purpose of making sure that the home you contracted to buy is still the home you're closing on. Every now and then there has been damage between the contract and closing, or the seller removed items that were supposed to be included in the transfer.

Congratulations, and it's time to get that tenant installed and the cash flowing.

Chapter 13

Property Management & Vendor Selection

Whether you're buying your first real estate investment property or you're a seasoned veteran, there are a lot of balls to juggle to successfully manage properties and get that cash flow into the bank. Starting out, it's usually self-management, but success brings growth. That's the goal, growth of your portfolio, cash flow and wealth.

Growth will eventually, usually sooner than you expect, require using outside help for management. Even in the beginning, certain things are not going to be in your areas of expertise, like plumbing, electrical and other repairs and maintenance. Even if you know how to do some things, time is a problem as well. So, let's get ready to hire someone for almost every phase of your property management business … except counting the money!

Don't let this chapter intimidate you if you're new to real estate investment. These are all things that you'll need to deal with at some point, but definitely not from day-1. Knowing what's coming with growth will allow you to begin an organized process of locating and selecting the help you'll need as your business grows.

Legal

While we all hope to have no need for lawyers, it's a fact of life that we'll need to draft documents and leases that protect us and conform to the legalities of our business and where we live. And, whether we want it or not, even a blue-chip tenant stops paying their rent now and then.

In some states attorneys can be certified in certain specialties. If that's the case where you live, look for attorneys certified in real estate and landlord/tenant relations. If there isn't a structured certification, there will still be attorneys who advertise that they specialize in real estate law, and you should locate several and talk to them to find one who fits your style and meets your needs. There will be more on this in the next chapter on tenant relations.

It would help going into attorney interviews if you at least have a basic knowledge of your state's landlord/tenant laws. A quick Google search on your state using a search phrase like this: "YourState .gov landlord tenant law" will turn up the state site in most cases. Here's what came up for Tennessee.

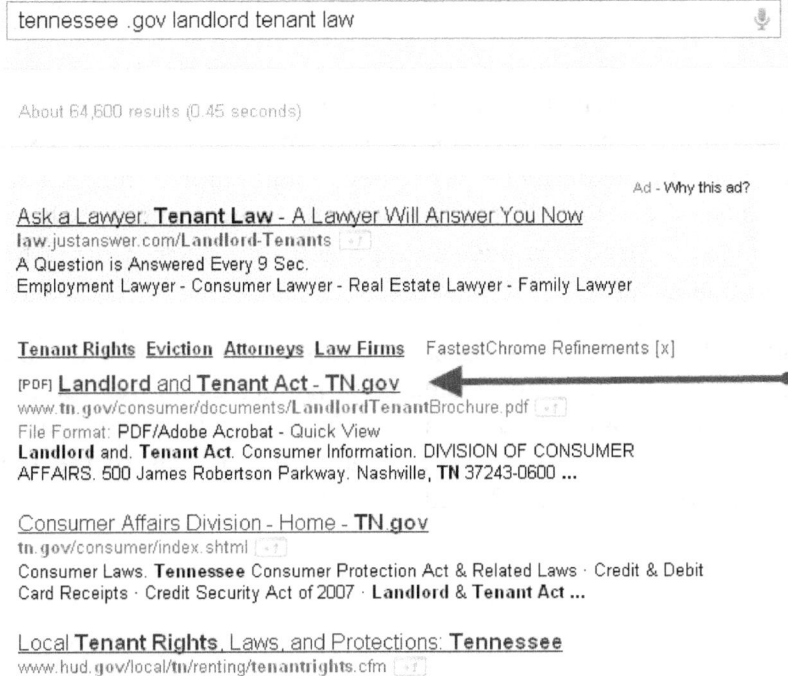

Accounting & Taxes

Real estate investment returns are leveraged by tax deferred exchanges and tax deduction strategies. Real estate is one of the more complex areas of tax law, so you may want an accountant for advice even before your first purchase.

In previous chapters we've discussed the advantages of depreciation deductions and other tax deferral and avoidance strategies, and you'll want to factor tax advantage into your investment return projections. To do this, you'll need a clear picture of the tax strategies available to you in your specific financial situation. That's where your accountant comes in.

Like attorneys, accountants may also advertise a specialization or dedication to certain types of businesses or clients. Interview until you locate one who has experience with real estate and a number of investor clients. As with all tax accounting, you want a balance between aggressive strategies and an approach that doesn't bring the IRS down on you.

Your accountant will eventually become a critical participant in your business, as the tax law is complicated and changes every year. While you could be a do-it-yourselfer in this area, it's certainly not advisable. Here's just a partial screen shot of the Table of Contents of the IRS Publication 527 for Residential Rental Property.

Publication 527 (2010), Residential Rental Property

(Including Rental of Vacation Homes)

For use in preparing *2010* Returns

Table of Contents

[image: irsrental]

It's deep reading, and not a productive activity when you can be using the time to locate and evaluate your next real estate investment.

Routine Maintenance – Minor Repairs

This is the category of maintenance and repairs that can normally be done by a general handyman, the jack-of-all-trades type. This can be one of the most important people on your management team. Usually your property manager will employ a handyman. A reliable on-call handyman can improve tenant relations by speeding minor repairs, and will help you to avoid higher cost repairs with routine maintenance and upkeep.

- windows and screens
- doors & hinges
- minor painting jobs
- simple electrical & plumbing repairs
- minor deck & wood repairs
- blind & curtain replacement
- changing filters in heating & cooling equipment
- minor cleaning of heating & cooling equipment

You may need to have two of these type of people on call unless you own enough properties to become the top customer on the list. The key is to jump on minor things to avoid the chance that they'll become major, and to avoid tenant complaints.

Specialty & Complex Repairs

These are repairs that require a higher skill level and more specialized tools and equipment. Plumbing, major drain cleaning, electrical re-wiring and circuit box repairs, heating and air conditioning work, roof work, and other more demanding repairs.

These are the kind of repairs that can be costly and cut investment return significantly. You'll want to have major equipment maintained to prolong its life and reduce the number of emergency repair callouts. These items, when they fail, also cause tenant dissatisfaction if they're not repaired quickly.

If you can find a reliable and reasonably priced company, they will probably offer some type of regular inspection program for major equipment. They normally offer a discount and priority on repairs for their regular inspection customers.

Major Renovation & Rehab

We're teaching blue-chip investment and buying well-kept properties, but sometimes you might want to plan upgrades to enhance the value of the property or avoid functional obsolescence. In these cases, you don't want a repair contractor. You probably want a general contractor who can call in sub-contractors, pull all necessary permits, and supervise the work.

The right general contractor who you trust can also help you with purchase decisions. If you have doubts about a home in your due diligence phase, you can call this contractor and ask them to take a look at it with you. Sometimes, investors use a general contractor as an inspector, as the homes they're considering are well cared for, but they want an expert to advise them on the overall structure and major components. The general contractor can also help you to make renovation decisions.

When a Big Job is Required

Actually, any repair job that's more than minor maintenance should not be started without some written confirmation of what's to be done and what's to be considered a satisfactory outcome. Whether an estimate of cost is part of it or not, both you and the repair person should have exactly the same expectations going in.

However, when it comes to more major work, such as major comfort equipment replacement or renovation projects, a more detailed contract and description of the work to be performed is an absolute must. The description of the work to be performed may not rise to the level of a full set of specifications, but it should at least accurately describe what is to be done and how it should look and perform after completion.

Many times the contract or work order will be supplied by the contractor. By design, it will favor their interests, and be very clear about how they get paid. However, read it carefully and make sure that it also allows a detailed description of the work to be performed, duration of phases and when the project should be finished, as well as how payments are related to the completion of each phase.

Zoning and permit compliance is a part of the contract, and should be of importance to the owner/investor. Failure of a contractor to pull the appropriate permits and pass inspections could result in problems from weeks to years later.

The Management Company Solution

Definitely at some point in your business growth you'll be investigating companies that specialize in property management. These companies take over all aspects of rental property management for a fee, generally a percentage of rents.

When Do You Bring In Outside Management?

The easy answer is "you'll probably know." If you're not getting along with tenants, or you find yourself setting a lower rent because you don't want to deal with a vacancy, or you are falling short in other areas because of the time you're spending on management tasks, then it's probably time. Also if you live outside the area you're investing in, then you'll definitely want a local property manager.

With many sources showing that property management company percentage charges are hovering between 7% and 10%(10% is pretty normal, less on larger purchase price or with a volume discount), you'll need to factor that into your decision. One good approach is to start out with this number built into your first and in every rental. As long as you're self-managing, you can consider it your salary of sorts. However, once you do make the decision to hire property management, you already have it covered.

What They Do

A property management company should take all of the normal management tasks off your plate. Of course, the management agreement should spell out who does what, and the level of decision-making authority you're willing to give up to the management company.

Your selection of a management company should be the end result of a careful and detailed investigation of their business practices and performance. Cost is a consideration, but it doesn't take long to lose a 1% savings in management fees to litigation costs with tenants or vendors.

Marketing, Budgeting & Financial

The property management person or company that you hire should have a thorough knowledge of the local rental market. Appropriate rents can't be set unless the competition is researched and the ratio of supply to demand is understood.

Right along with that knowledge, the management company should be on top of expenses and budgeting. One advantage that can come from using a property management solution is that they will have vendors working on a volume basis, thus lowering costs in some cases.

Marketing is an expense, and any method or knowledge that cuts the cost while maintaining a supply of renters is a good thing. An experienced property management company will know what marketing and advertising works best in the area, and will fill vacant units faster.

Professional property management can help with tax decisions as well. They provide bookkeeping services and even tax accounting if desired in some cases. Having a structured budget and a plan can result in end-of-year tax strategies to save money.

Tenant Management

Once tenants are in place, there are a myriad of tasks and responsibilities to not only comply with landlord/tenant laws, but also to keep tenants happy and increase occupancy time. Tenant relations is a big part of the management function, and doing it right will cut vacancy and credit loss.

On the negative side, when delinquent rent collection or eviction is required, the property management company will be up to date on all laws and procedural deadlines. They'll normally have an attorney to call with questions as well.

Facility Management & Maintenance

There is also an opportunity to save money in this area due to "economy of scale." That's because the property management company will have staff or regular contractors and vendors to handle landscaping, maintenance, cleaning, repairs and renovation. They'll give priority to the management company's properties, and normally work for a less expensive negotiated rate.

Contracts with vendors can produce a better budgeting situation, as fixed rates or quoted rate ranges can be negotiated. A repair company will cut emergency rates in exchange for long term contracts that provide work during slow periods.

Regular scheduled maintenance on heating and cooling equipment can be less expensive on a contract, reduce emergency breakdowns, and result in lower hourly and repair pricing from vendors. This will normally also come with priority in busy seasonal times, reducing tenant complaints while waiting to have problems repaired.

Administration & Risk Management

Paperwork is something none of us relish, but it's a major part of the administration of a property rental business. Property management companies have procedures, filing systems, and software/hardware specifically developed for the property management business. Checks get cut more quickly, bills get paid on time, and rents get collected and deposited.

There are always reporting requirements, whether they be from local and municipal governments or the IRS. All interactions with tenants should be documented for legal and liability reasons. State laws are normally very rigid when it comes to the handling of tenant deposits and rents. Business risk is reduced when all of these documentation tasks are done properly and in a timely manner.

In the next chapter we'll talk about tenant selection and management in detail. Part of that discussion will be centered around legal and risk considerations. It's important enough to deserve an entire chapter, and shouldn't intimidate you ... just prepare you so that you can realize your investment goals.

The Property Management Agreement

Landlord and tenant relations are subject to significant regulations in most states due to a history of problems with disputes, as well as property management's failure to adequately account for funds income and dispersal. The Property Management Agreement is the document signed by the property owner and the management company setting out the responsibilities of each.

If you're working with a Realtor® who manages properties, which may be required in some areas, there will likely be a standardized management agreement that is provided by the Realtor Association. It will be worded to be fair to both parties and set out a clear description of duties and compensation.

The structure of one of these agreements can help us to illustrate the many considerations involved in property management. Let's take a look at the major sections of one state's mandated property management agreement for Realtors.

Parties, Property, Term

The agreement will clearly identify the parties involved. The property will be identified by address and legal description in some cases. Most state laws require a definite stated period of time for the agreement to be in force, though some may allow a clause that sets up an automated renewal at the end of the term for another stated period.

Obligations of Property Manager

This section can be broken out into sub-sections covering collection of rents, how funds are to be deposited and where, as well as language covering:

- rental agreement & lease signing, renewal and termination
- probable requirement for a trust account where funds are deposited and strictly accounted for
- owner's obligation to provide funds when circumstances such as repairs create a shortfall in the account
- accounting procedures, how the property manager will account for expenditures and income for the owner's examination and records, as well as for the state regulation department

The language in this section should make it clear as to what the property manager is required to do.

Grant of Authority

In this section of the agreement, the owner grants the authority to the property manager to carry out their duties. The owner specifically acknowledges the authority of the manager to advertise, maintain and repair, negotiate certain maintenance contracts, engage others to perform services, and recover possession for non-payment or other default reasons.

Compensation

This section outlines how and how much the property manager will be paid. There can be multiple methods in one agreement that vary by the type of duties or their complexity. Most agreements are for a stated percentage of rents collected.

There can be language in this section stating liquidation payments if the agreement is terminated early for any reason.

Hold Harmless & Insurance Clauses

This clause holds the property manager harmless for liability, lawsuits or costs in connection with the management of the property if these result from owner negligence.

The insurance clause states that the owner will at all times maintain required and sufficient liability and property damage insurance. There could be state minimums in this regard.

Compliance With Laws

Both parties agree in this section to comply with all laws and regulations related to the property and landlord tenant relations laws. There may be a mention of environmental hazards and laws related to them in this section as well, such as the requirement to provide proper disclosure of lead based paint hazards. We'll look into this in more detail in the next chapter.

Deposits Procedures

This section clarifies the amount of deposits to be collected from tenants, how and where they'll be held in deposit, and procedures for refund or withholding of deposits if there is damage or other problems.

Other & Miscellaneous

Procedures for disputes between the owner and the property manager will be outlined here. Mediation or arbitration may be required before litigation. Who pays attorney fees if damages are awarded to one of the parties is also a part of most agreements, as well as the statement that the laws of the state in which the agreement is executed will determine actions and results.

Though these agreements and the many considerations involved in rental property management may seem daunting, they're followed every day for millions of rental properties without any lawsuits or problems.

Chapter 14

Tenant Marketing & Selection

Whether it's you or a property management company doing the work, getting and keeping good tenants makes a huge difference in the profitability of your real estate investments. From the first advertisement through the expiration of the lease, there are a number of critical factors contributing to the tenant experience and your return on investment.

Marketing Plan

Marketing and advertising are often confused or considered the same thing. However, marketing is a process that presents and promotes products or services and solicits their purchase by the consumer or target market segment. Marketing includes ideas and strategy, while advertising is an implementation of some of those strategies.

Advertising takes ideas and product/service features and benefits and places them in front of prospective customers. You or your property manager should have at least a basic marketing plan that includes not only how you're going to advertise, but how you will incentivize tenants to remain through multiple lease periods. If you're in a strong market, blue-chip properties may not need any incentives to keep tenants, but it's good to have something figured out just in case.

Marketing for rental real estate can include:

- Curb appeal of the property
- Advertising the neighborhood amenities
- Advertising the home amenities and features
- Maintenance procedures for tenant satisfaction
- Tenant surveys & your responses
- Incentives to renew leases
- Tenant parties or promotions

Marketing, as the image indicates, is the roof over your approach for overall presentation, pricing, and advertising that creates a demand for your product, a rental home. Advertising is one piece, but there are many ways in which you can influence the prospective tenant's perception of the value of your property.

Let's look at some of the elements in your overall business and property management to see how they can be a part of a comprehensive marketing plan to position your property(ies) as desirable and preferable to your target market tenants.

Blue-chip as a Marketing Concept

We've been talking until now about the blue-chip real estate investment concept as your strategy for long term profit with lower risk and a higher return than one would realize on less expensive properties.

As we've thoroughly discussed the reasons why blue-chip properties rent for more, experience lower vacancy and credit loss costs, and realize greater appreciation, it's logical that our target tenants will place a value on them for some of the same reasons.

- They're in better condition than the normal rental.
- They're in better neighborhoods.
- Functionally, they're more modern than others.

So, we now have the first component in our marketing plan … blue-chip. Call it that or any other marketable term that will appeal to the tenant who is willing to spend more for rent on a blue-chip type property.

Your advertising, wherever it's placed, will use wording and images that create a blue-chip image, an above-the-norm rental home. You'll promote the neighborhood, stable neighbors, pleasing neighborhood characteristics, schools, etc. All of this of course implies that it will cost more to rent this home than the normal run-of-the-mill competition.

Advertising

Now that we have a marketing plan and approach, we can decide how to fulfill the plan and fill our units through the use of selective advertising that is very focused on our target tenant and market. Wasting money in advertising is easy if you don't know who your target customer is and what message you want to deliver. However, we've determined those things, so now we just need to reach the desired prospect with our advertising.

In the last ten years, advertising has changed dramatically as the Internet developed, and we have adopted smaller computers, smart phones, and social networks. This is definitely a positive development, as you can now better target your desired prospect, and it's less expensive than when we were locked into print, TV, or radio.

Let's run through some old tried-and-true advertising methods and media as well as some new ways in which you can advertise your rental properties in a way that targets the best prospect at the right time and gives them the appropriate information to seek your properties out.

Newspaper

It hardly seems necessary to mention newspaper classified and display ads as effective for rental property advertising. They still work because people still read newspapers and go to the classifieds to search for their next rental home.

Classified ads are inexpensive if you keep the number of words under control, and you can use words that appeal to your target tenant prospect. Using words that build an expectation of homes with upscale amenities and in the best neighborhoods will bring calls from tenants who value these factors and will pay for them.

Later in this chapter we'll talk about fair housing laws and you can use the information there to steer clear of any possible words or statements that may run afoul of federal or state laws. That will apply not only to newspaper advertisements, but any other media we'll talk about here.

Craigslist

$825 / 2br - 900ft² - Newly remodeled single family home. - (Sandia High School Area)

$775 / 3br - 1500ft² - Rio Rancho North Meadows house 3br2ba2cg Discounted Rent - (RR-North Meadows) pic

$1575 / 5br - 2800ft² - Great Neighborhood!Possible Rent to Own. Backyard access - (Tramway/Montgomery) pic

$1200 / 3br - 1850ft² - Great Home in La Cueva School District - (8117 Curry Ave.) pic

$685 / 3br - Quite Peaceful Neighborhood - Own dxo fiu - (albuquerque)

$950 / 2br - 1300ft² - Beautiful Adobe Home - (near downtown, river, s. valley) pic

$1000 / 3br - 1670ft² - clean 3bdrm2bth house - (rio rancho) pic

$750 / 2br - 850ft² - Beautiful, Modern Old Town Home - (Old Town - Downtown)

$1000 / 3br - 1460ft² - Old Town, Downtown, close to UNM remodeled Home - (Old Town) pic

$330 Efficiency Unit - (1339 San Mateo SE) pic

$1950 / 4br - Gorgeous Nob Hill Home! - (Nob Hill, Ridgecrest Neighborhood, UNM) pic

$935 / 1350ft² - New Carpet and Paint Throughout - (Near San Pedro & Candelaria NE)

$900 / 3br - 1200ft² - NW Home - (Montano and Unser (Albu)) pic

We're jumping a little out of sequence here in media for advertising because Craigslist is really an online classified advertising media. The same wording, features and benefits you advertise in the newspaper will work on Craigslist, and it's free!

Craigslist is better for the tenant looking for your property because they can search on a variety of words and phrases that will pop up your listing. And, because it's free, you can have a longer description with your keywords and phrases, as well as photos.

Don't forget that people run ads on Craigslist about what they want as well. You can search for ads looking for a rental in neighborhoods where you have properties. If you keep tabs on ads like these, you can actually be contacting prospective tenants when you get a move-out notice and have a tenant ready to move in immediately.

Association Newsletters

Subdivisions and many neighborhoods put out printed or email newsletters to residents, and some of them take advertisements to offset costs. These can be an excellent advertising resource, as residents often have relatives, friends or acquaintances who would like to live in the neighborhood but aren't in the market to buy a home.

Bulletin Boards

Whether you're renting in a college area or near a large employer, you may be able to post rental ads on their bulletin boards for free. This is very targeted, as you're advertising to people who want to live in the area close to their jobs or where they attend classes.

On the fringes of the nicer neighborhoods there are frequently upscale markets, green grocers and other businesses catering to the area residents. If they allow you to post your ads on their bulletin boards, you'll be reaching non-residents who shop there and may want to live closer.

Website or Blog

With the tools and resources available today, there's no reason you can't have a custom website just for your properties. It allows you to use as many high quality photos and as much text as necessary to promote your rental units.

You can do it for free using WordPress.com, which allows you to create a normal website or a blog, or a combination of both. WordPress hosts your site, and you can buy a "dummies" book and be up and running in days with only the cost of the book out of pocket. Of course, as your business grows, you can do something more extensive, but it's not necessary, especially at the beginning.

Social Networks

It's a whole new advertising world, with "relationship marketing" one of the new buzz words. Building a website is a type of billboard, but you need drive-by traffic so they'll see it and respond. Another approach, either stand-alone or to help promote your website would be a Facebook page. It's free and easy to build, and will allow you to begin to promote your units to a growing base of prospects, as well as past and present tenants.

You begin to interact with visitors to your page, talking about the local area and your properties. Every time you do an improvement, you can announce it on your Facebook page. Use Twitter, another free resource, as well. There are people right now searching Twitter with phrases like "YourTown rental homes."

Some Facebook Statistics

- More than 950 million active users
- More than 50% log on every day
- Average user has 130 Friends
- Average user is connected to 80 community pages, groups and events

- On average, more than 250 million photos are uploaded every day
- More than 350 million active users access Facebook with mobile devices

You'll spend a couple of days setting up the free Twitter and Facebook accounts, but after that they don't require a lot of your time. You post when you have something to say, or when someone asks a question. You can receive notices from Facebook when someone sends you a message.

There's a new social network on the block as I write this, Google Plus, or Google+. You can build a free business page there in just a few minutes. It can contain all the text you want to place there, as well as photos and videos of your properties. Don't overlook video as a marketing tool for rental homes.

Tenant Interview and Selection

Now that you've developed a successful marketing plan and placed your advertising, you'll begin to receive tenant interest and applications. As your Internet and social network advertising is running continuously, you'll be getting applicants when you don't have availability, but you can build a file and get their contact information for later.

Fair Housing & What You Can & Can't Do

Note in the text below that's taken directly from the HUD.gov site, the first paragraph (in bold for emphasis) states that there can be some things an owner can do in an owner-occupied building or in single family situations that others can't. However, you should know these things and consult an attorney if you're unsure of what to do or say.

Following in italics is from the HUD.gov site:

What Housing Is Covered?

The Fair Housing Act covers most housing. **In some circumstances, the Act exempts owner-occupied buildings with no more than four units, single-family housing sold or rented without the use of a broker,** *and housing operated by organizations and private clubs that limit occupancy to members.*

What Is Prohibited?

In the Sale and Rental of Housing: No one may take any of the following actions based on race, color, national origin, religion, sex, familial status or handicap:

- *Refuse to rent or sell housing*
- *Refuse to negotiate for housing*
- *Make housing unavailable*
- *Deny a dwelling*
- *Set different terms, conditions or privileges for sale or rental of a dwelling*
- *Provide different housing services or facilities*
- *Falsely deny that housing is available for inspection, sale, or rental*

- *For profit, persuade owners to sell or rent (blockbusting) or*
- *Deny anyone access to or membership in a facility or service (such as a multiple listing service) related to the sale or rental of housing.*

In Mortgage Lending: No one may take any of the following actions based on race, color, national origin, religion, sex, familial status or handicap (disability):

- *Refuse to make a mortgage loan*
- *Refuse to provide information regarding loans*
- *Impose different terms or conditions on a loan, such as different interest rates, points, or fees*
- *Discriminate in appraising property*
- *Refuse to purchase a loan or*
- *Set different terms or conditions for purchasing a loan.*

In Addition: It is illegal for anyone to:

- *Threaten, coerce, intimidate or interfere with anyone exercising a fair housing right or assisting others who exercise that right*
- *Advertise or make any statement that indicates a limitation or preference based on race, color, national origin, religion, sex, familial status, or handicap. This prohibition against discriminatory advertising applies to single-family and owner-occupied housing that is otherwise exempt from the Fair Housing Act.*

Additional Protection if You Have a Disability

If you or someone associated with you:

- *Have a physical or mental disability (including hearing, mobility and visual impairments, chronic alcoholism, chronic mental illness, AIDS, AIDS Related Complex and mental retardation) that substantially limits one or more major life activities*
- *Have a record of such a disability or*
- *Are regarded as having such a disability*

*your landlord **may not:***

- *Refuse to let you make reasonable modifications to your dwelling or common use areas, at your expense, if necessary for the disabled person to use the housing. (Where reasonable, the landlord may permit changes only if you agree to restore the property to its original condition when you move.)*
- *Refuse to make reasonable accommodations in rules, policies, practices or services if necessary for the disabled person to use the housing.*

Example: A building with a no pets policy must allow a visually impaired tenant to keep a guide dog.

Example: An apartment complex that offers tenants ample, unassigned parking must honor a request from a mobility-impaired tenant for a reserved space near her apartment if necessary to assure that she can have access to her apartment.

However, housing need not be made available to a person who is a direct threat to the health or safety of others or who currently uses illegal drugs.

Once you're using a professional management company, they should be up-to-date on all of the current laws and regulations. This is good information for you to know until then, even if you just own a couple of single family homes.

The Phone Call or Email of Interest

In your initial contact with a potential tenant, you want to keep the legal stuff in mind and take a business-like approach. However, you'll want to be friendly and not over-inquisitive. You can ask a few general questions, and answer a few about the home. If you didn't advertise price, this will probably be one of their first questions, and a way to quickly end a call if it's more than they can afford.

The Showing Appointment

If you're going to show a rental property, make sure that someone knows when you'll be there, and you have arranged a distress call word so you can quickly reach them with your cell phone to let them know there's a problem.

Let your prospective tenants precede you into the home, and walk around without you hovering, as they may want to discuss things without fear of insulting or annoying you. Don't set up multiple showings at the same time or too close together. It may seem like a good idea to build a little competitive thing with multiple renters there at once, but it makes it impossible to work with them individually and to select the best.

The Tenant Application & Processing

HUD, the Department of Housing & Urban Development, provides a sample tenant application. The site states that it's just a sample, and you should only use it in conjunction with an attorney's advice and modifications to meet the legalities of your state and to comply with any new laws.

Sorry, it's a very long link, but you can go to http://hudnsphelp.info and search on "sample tenant rental application form" and go right to it.

Let's go through the major sections of the form to see what HUD says a tenant should be providing for information.

Occupant Information

This information is required for each occupant of the property:

- Complete name
- Relationship to head of household
- Male or female
- Birth date
- Whether they're a student or not
- Social Security Number

Current Address Information

Get a current primary and alternate phone number or cell phone number.

Type of Property

This is an application from prospective tenants without a specified property, and asks their property requirements, size, bedrooms, baths, etc. While you may be taking applications for a specific property, you won't select every applicant, and this information can be kept on file in case you get a chance to contact them with another available home.

Housing References

This application asks for 3 years of housing history, with the name, address and phone number of the landlord or lender if owned, as well as the dates of occupancy.

Personal & Family References

Though not a part of this sample document, very important to your rent collection efforts is a requirement for family & business references with address and phone information. These should be people who would be likely to know the whereabouts of your tenants after they move out.

Household Information

This section wants to know about anyone that isn't in the first section as a full-time occupant who may reside in the unit temporarily during the lease:

- children temporarily absent
- joint custody arrangements
- children away at school
- children in the process of being adopted
- other temporarily absent family members

Other questions, such as if the number of household members is expected to change during the lease, and any record of criminal convictions of any member of the household. Details of convictions, dates, city, county, state and whether a felony are also asked.

This section also asks about previous evictions or bankruptcies, with details and dates, as well as why they are moving. For your marketing, also ask how they came to hear about your property.

Income Information

Income sources and amounts are required here for every member of the household who has an income from:

- wages and salaries
- self-employment
- unemployment benefits or worker's compensation
- public assistance
- child support or alimony
- social security payments
- pension payments
- disability payments
- educational assistance income
- annuities of any type
- any other income sources not listed and amounts

Of course, the goal here is to be sure that they can afford the rent based on regular and reasonably secure income sources. A good rule of thumb is to make sure the annual household income is at least 40 times the monthly rent.

Credit Sources

Get their credit card accounts, mortgage lenders, vehicle loans and other credit information here. You or a hired tenant screening company will be checking credit and getting a credit score. They must give permission in writing, which you can place here or at the end of the application just above their signatures.

Asset Information

In this section they should identify their assets, such as vehicles owned, any other real estate, bank checking and savings accounts, certificates of deposit, trust funds, pension and retirement accounts, life insurance, annuities and cash on hand.

For credit checks, for any financed assets get the lender's contact information and the account number.

This section can also ask about personal property, especially furniture and items to be placed in the rental home. It can also advise them, though the lease will require it, that they should have a value for these assets in order to purchase adequate renter's insurance.

Vehicle Information

Separate from the financial asset information for vehicle ownership, get their make, model and license plate information in this section.

Signatures and Permissions

At the end of the document, you'll be getting signatures and dates signed. Just above those, you'll have some text that may be similar to this text at the end of the HUD sample application:

I certify that all information and answers to the questions are true and complete to the best of my knowledge. I consent to release the necessary information to determine my eligibility. I understand that providing false information or making false statements may be grounds for denial of my application. I also understand that such action may result in criminal penalties.

I consent to have management verify the information contained in this application for purposes of proving my eligibility for occupancy. I will provide all necessary information and expedite this process in any way possible. I understand that my occupancy is contingent on meeting management's resident selection criteria.

I understand that in compliance with the FAIR CREDIT REPORTING ACT the processing of this application includes but is not limited to making any inquiries deemed necessary to verify the accuracy of the information I provided, including procuring consumer reports from consumer credit reporting agencies and obtaining credit information from other credit institutions.

I hereby grant this property owner and _____
[Insert Management Company Name] the right to process this application for the purpose of obtaining a Rental/Lease Agreement with this property. Additionally, I authorize all corporations, companies, law enforcement agencies, academic institutions, and current and former employers to release information they may have about me and release them from any liability and responsibility from doing so. A photographic or faxed copy of this authorization shall be as valid as the original.

This information is to help you to select a tenant application form, perhaps from an online source or office supply. This should be a minimum of what you want to collect for information, and you should have an attorney review your application prior to using it. Ask your attorney up front, as they may have one they've prepared prior that is ready to go for your state.

Based on the information in your applications, you'll make a tenant selection and offer them the home. The thorough nature of your application and selection process should minimize rent collection and eviction issues, but there's always the possibility that you'll have to initiate collection or eviction actions later. In the next chapter we'll look at a sample lease agreement and procedures for moving tenants in, moving them out, and handling deposits and damages.

Chapter 15

The Lease & Tenant Management

In the previous chapter we looked at the tenant selection process. Even if you're using a property manager, it's good to have an understanding of the lease and the leasing process.

You have your tenant selected, and they're ready to sign a lease and move in. The development of a thorough and clear lease agreement and move-in/move-out procedures will go a long way toward avoiding future hassles, deposit disputes, and legal problems.

You can find plenty of free and inexpensive lease agreements on the Web, as evidenced by just a few of 25 million results in a Google search for "state legal lease agreement."

state legal lease agreement

About 25,100,000 results (0.34 seconds)

Using one or more of these choices and some research into your state's landlord tenant law, you can probably come up with a lease that will work for you. However, you'll still want to run it by an attorney experienced in your state's laws.

Landlord tenant laws in many states have become quite detailed because of tenant complaints and legal disputes in the past. As an example of the complexity of some of these statutes, here are the title headings in the first three Articles in the Arizona Residential Landlord & Tenant Act.

ARTICLE 1.
GENERAL PROVISIONS

ARTICLE 2.
LANDLORD OBLIGATIONS
Section
§ 33-1321. Security deposits
§ 33-1322. Disclosure and tender of written rental
agreement
§ 33-1323. Landlord to supply possession of
dwelling unit
§ 33-1324. Landlord to maintain fit premises
§ 33-1325. Limitation of liability
§ 33-1329. Regulation of rents; authority
§ 33-1330. Transfer of records on sale
§ 33-1331. Notice of foreclosure; effect on lease;damages

ARTICLE 3.
TENANT OBLIGATIO)S
Section
§ 33-1341. Tenant to maintain dwelling unit
§ 33-1342. Rules and regulations
§ 33-1343. Access
§ 33-1344. Tenant to use and occupy as a
dwelling unit

As you can see, before they even get to the articles for Remedies and other parts of the Act, there is a lot of detail here. They get into the process in depth, right down to bedbugs rules.

It is probably a good idea for you to look up online your state's landlord tenant law, or get a copy if they don't have it online. If nothing else, it can illustrate the value of an experienced attorney's advice and approval of your lease form and procedures. You'll want procedures for move-in and move-out and want to run them by your attorney as well. The rules, procedures, notices and deadlines for past due rent and eviction will be spelled out in the law.

The Lease Agreement

Laws vary significantly from state to state. As one example, in some states it's legal for a tenant to withhold rent while repairs that effect living conditions, like heating, are made. In many states it's not legal. It's best that a lease agreement specifically address issues like the withholding of rent for non-performance of repairs. Tenants should be fully aware of what they can and cannot do, and what could result in an eviction action.

In viewing sample lease agreements from different states, some or all of the items we'll list here may be a part of the agreement. Most of them will, but the terms and explanations related to the items may be different.

Parties and Property

The landlord and tenant, addresses, and the address and/or legal description of the property will be at the top of the agreement.

Payment of Rent and Lease Term

The amount of the rent, when it's due, the beginning and ending of the lease term will all be here. Any monetary late charges and description of the deadline dates for late charges must be spelled out.

This section should also spell out collection procedures that will be put into play and at how many days late they will start. Depending on state law, some leases have a set late fee dollar amount at an example 5 day period, then after 10-15 days extra late fees begin to accrue. This is also where the lease can provide for a fee for returned checks.

The tenant should be instructed in this section to never pay rent in cash unless they immediately receive a receipt from the landlord, or you can require a check or money order. This will preclude any possibility of a tenant claiming to have paid rent when they haven't.

Tenants should be instructed here or elsewhere in the lease that notice, typically 30 days, is required in writing before move-out. There can also be a statement in this area about abandoned personal property and how it will be disposed of and when.

Property Inspection at Move-in and Move-out

This is an area in which disputes arise often. This section of the lease should be as detailed as necessary to make it very clear as to the amount of deposits, how they'll be held, if interest is to be paid on deposits, and what conditions might cause the withholding of deposits after move-out. It should be very clear as well as to when the landlord must refund deposits after move-out.

In this section the description of what constitutes "normal wear and tear" versus damages for which the tenant is liable, will be detailed. This is where the move-in and move-out condition checklist will be mentioned. It is important to have a landlord representative and the tenant go through every room and the exterior of the property and note the condition it's in at move-in in detail. Then, the same form is used again at move-out to contrast the condition.

A clear understanding of what constitutes "normal wear and tear," and what "damage" is will lessen the incidence of disputes when you want to hold back a portion of damage deposits for repairs.

Example: The statement that minor wall scratches and wall hanging hook or mounting holes are normal, while a hole in the wall requiring sheetrock or plaster repair is damage subject to withholding of a portion of the damage deposit.

The condition checklist will have the signatures of landlord and tenant and a handwritten entry by the tenant of the condition of each line item on the form. The column for move-in and then again at move-out are next to each other allowing an easy comparison of condition in each case.

Encourage the tenant to write down anything they see and in detail. There may need to be additional sheets with a reference from the item to more detail. Hopefully there's going to be little or nothing to write down during move-in, but your tenant will want to record anything that could result in a damage claim when they leave.

ITEM	CONDITION ON ARRIVAL	CONDITION ON DEPARTURE
LIVING ROOM		
Floor & Floor Covering		
Walls & Ceiling		
Door(s)		
Door Lock(s) & Hardware		
Lighting Fixture(s)		
Window(s) & Screen(s)		
Window Covering(s)		
Smoke Detector &/or CO Detector		
Fireplace		
Other		
KITCHEN		
Floor & Floor Coverings		
Walls & Ceiling		
Door(s)		
Door Lock(s) and Hardware		
Window(s) & Screen(s)		

The image shows a portion of a checklist and how the tenant will make an entry next to each item room-by-room, and for the exterior as well with a home.

The proper explanations in the lease for how this form will be used, and making sure that the tenant understands its importance will help you to avoid problems at move-out. The tenant should be encouraged to write up anything they see before move-in that is a condition issue, no matter how minor. That way they go into the lease with a comfort level that they have an input into the process.

When they move out, they can go through the process again, seeing exactly what they wrote the first time. They'll not refute what they did at move-in, and they'll be less likely to dispute deposit issues related to damage.

It isn't a bad idea to take photos during or before the walk-through, with your digital camera time and date stamping them. This gives you a record of the condition, and photos can be taken again during the move-out walkthrough.

Security and Damage Deposits

The lease will indicate the amount of deposits to be paid by the tenant, and what the deposit is for:

- Security deposit – depending on state law, this may be a single month's rent, first and last, or some other amount.
- Damage deposit – again, state law will probably dictate a maximum amount that can be held as a damage deposit.
- Pet deposit – if an extra deposit is allowed for a pet, but this could be a non-refundable pet cleaning fee instead.

In the section discussing deposits, there should be very clear instructions as to whether interest will be paid, how long after move-out the landlord has to refund deposits, and how any damage will be documented as well as the cost to repair. Many states require deposits to be held in a separate account from landlord personal funds, and may specify that interest be paid.

This section should also instruct the tenant that they must provide a forwarding address at move-out in order to receive any deposit refunds via a check in the mail.

Tenant Duties or Agreements

Here are some of the items in a lease which are the duties of the tenant, and their signature indicates their agreement:

- **Use of property** – this is a general statement that the property is for residential use only, and that the tenant will not allow others to use it for any non-residential or illegal purpose.

- **Notice of absence** – requires that the tenant notify the landlord in writing if the unit is to be left unoccupied for an extended period, such as 30 days or more.
- **Utilities waste** – tenant agrees to conserve utilities for which the landlord is paying. **Maintain premises and damages** – the tenant agrees to keep the home clean at all times, and not to abuse appliances, fixtures or any part of the property. This duplicates some of the content above about damages, so may not be necessary in this section.
- **Alterations** – most alterations will be prohibited without written approval of the landlord, and the tenant could be liable to restore the home to its original condition before move-out.
- **Noise** – tenants agree not to create a nuisance that would annoy neighbors, and to keep noise to a normal level.
- **Locks** – only the landlord can change or rekey locks unless written permission is given for the tenant to do so. If they do, the locks become the property of the landlord.
- **Subleasing** – normally this is not allowed, but could be OK under certain circumstances with the written approval of the landlord.
- **Permission to enter** – the tenant agrees to allow the landlord or landlord's agent to enter the property to inspect with reasonable prior notice, usually 24 hours.
- **Attached homeowner restrictions** – if there is a homeowner covenants and restrictions document for the subdivision, it should be attached and the tenant agrees to abide by those rules in addition to the lease requirements.
- **Parking** – tenant agrees to limitations on number of vehicles and where they can be parked.
- **Renter's insurance** – tenant agrees that landlord is not responsible for tenant personal property and that they will (or should) maintain a renter's insurance policy to cover the value of their property.

There will be other legal clauses related to default, severability, liability and abandonment, and most standard lease forms will cover them. However, have the form you want to use examined by your attorney.

Pre-1978 Homes & Lead Base Paint

Our blue-chip investing strategy doesn't encourage the purchase of older homes for maintenance and functional reasons mentioned before. However, if you do have a home built prior to 1978, the EPA, Environmental Protection Agency, requires a lead base paint disclosure form be presented to the tenants and signed before they enter into any other agreement to lease.

This form states whether the landlord/owner has any knowledge of lead base paint in the home, and allows the tenants to either have the home inspected or waive the inspection. The fine for failing to handle this properly is stiff, so make sure that it is signed and time/dated prior to the time and date of the lease agreement.

Management

Earlier in the book we looked at the improvement of return on investment when tenant turnover is reduced, and it is substantial. Good management practices can make the difference and make your tenants want to stay for more than just the initial lease period.

Clear Rules, Instructions & Follow-up

We've stressed that the lease should be very clear as to terms and the responsibilities of the tenant. Either in the lease or in other documents, they should be given instructions in reporting problems with the home, equipment or appliances. Whether it's via email, phone or another method, make sure that they know how and where to report any problems they have.

Rental property is a business, and your tenants will respect the fact that you operate in a business-like way. This would include being prompt and meeting all deadlines, even when letting them know about late rents or bounced checks.

Speedy Response and Correction/Repair

Concern for the comfort, good will, and safety of your tenants requires that you respond to their request for help quickly. If you've called a repair person, let them know and who you called. If there is a promised response time, tell them that as well and have them call you if the repair company isn't there when they're supposed to be.

Have repair people call you upon completion and give you the details and resolution of the repair. If it can't be completed due to waiting for parts or there's something more serious to deal with, get their best estimate of completion time and coordinate with the tenant. If it's ten degrees below zero and the furnace will be out of commission for two days, you'll need to put the tenant up elsewhere or provide temporary heat of some kind. Some contractors can bring in electric room heaters for this purpose.

Once all repairs are completed, follow up again with the tenant a day or so later to make sure that things are still operating properly. They'll appreciate it.

Keep Them Safe

You shouldn't leave maintenance of things like smoke detectors, carbon dioxide detectors, or other safety devices up to your tenants. Make an appointment every few months, go into the home, and replace batteries and check the operation of these devices. This illustrates your concern for their safety and takes one thing off their minds.

Document Everything in Writing

For both liability and tenant customer service reasons, everything you do and every communication with your tenants should be documented in writing. A multi-part form or follow-up emails can be used for this. You want your tenants to have a copy of all of your service work, battery replacements, etc.

Management Forms & Records

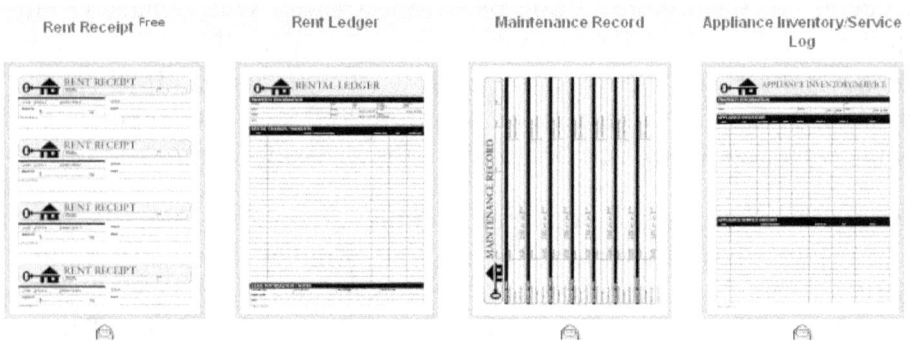

The image shows a few of many forms available from one website for landlords, but there are others. A Google search for "rental property management forms" should turn up some choices for you. Here's a blow-up of the Rent Ledger Form:

Preview Image   DOWNLOAD/PRINT   X

RENTAL LEDGER

PROPERTY INFORMATION

ADDRESS		UNIT	LATE FEE	OTHER CHARGES		MONTHLY RENT
TENANT		PHONE	- - ☐ CELL ☐ HOME	PHONE	- - ☐ CELL ☐ HOME	
TENANT		PHONE	- - ☐ CELL ☐ HOME	OTHER OCCUPANTS		
NOTES						

RENTAL CHARGES / PAYMENTS

DATE	CHARGE / PAYMENT DESCRIPTION	CHARGE / DUE	PAID	BALANCE DUE

LEASE INFORMATION / NOTES

LEASE START DATE	LEASE END DATE	LEASE RENEWAL	MOVE OUT DATE
OWNER / NOTES			
NOTES			

There are also online and software solutions for property management, possibly overkill until you have several properties though. However, if you like the online solution idea, here's a webpage with pricing and features at http://rentmonitor.com:

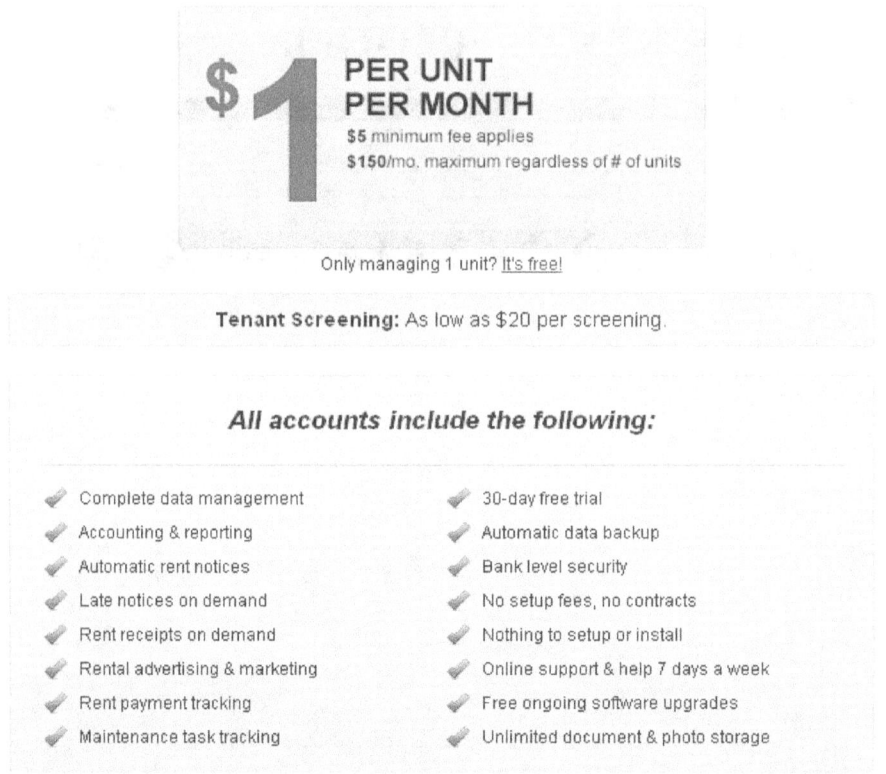

$1 PER UNIT PER MONTH
$5 minimum fee applies
$150/mo. maximum regardless of # of units

Only managing 1 unit? It's free!

Tenant Screening: As low as $20 per screening.

All accounts include the following:

Complete data management	30-day free trial
Accounting & reporting	Automatic data backup
Automatic rent notices	Bank level security
Late notices on demand	No setup fees, no contracts
Rent receipts on demand	Nothing to setup or install
Rental advertising & marketing	Online support & help 7 days a week
Rent payment tracking	Free ongoing software upgrades
Maintenance task tracking	Unlimited document & photo storage

Note that one unit is free, and two to five would be $5/month. There are other online solutions, and this isn't a recommendation, just an example. This service also does tenant screening which would allow you to avoid some of the background, reference and credit check duties. However, there are a large number of tenant screening services as well, all easily checked out with an online search.

If you have another business or you've used Quicken products before, you may prefer a software solution instead of online services.

Quicken Rental Property Manager 2012

Features and Benefits

What's New for 2012

System Requirements

Help and Support

See How it Works

Easily organize your personal and rental property finances

Key features and benefits:

- Includes everything in Quicken Home & Business, and more
- Organizes all your personal and rental property finances in one place
- Identifies tax-deductible rental property expenses
- Tracks income and expenses by property, and easily compare profit and loss

Quicken's Rental Property Manager software is around $150, but if you're a Quicken fan, you may find it to be your best approach, as it ties in personal accounting as well.

Most property management companies will use a software program such as PropertyWare. If you choose to employ a management company, try to get a good understanding on how the software or web application will communicate with you.

A thorough lease agreement and good tenant management will increase your return on investment over time. Start out right and the system you put in place can grow with you.

Chapter 16

The 1031 Exchange for Portfolio Growth

Blue-chip rental property investment is about holding properties for rental income, but at some point you may want to sell a property. Perhaps it's appreciated in value and there are other properties you can buy for better cash flow. Maybe you're noticing that the neighborhood is not as much in-demand as when you purchased the home.

Sometimes a property is doing well as a cash flow generator, but opportunities elsewhere are such that you can leverage by selling one and buying two. There are a number of reasons why you may decide to sell a property, and taxes are a factor as well as price and opportunity.

At the IRS.gov website, there is a section titled "Like-Kind Exchanges Under IRC Code Section 1031." With most investments like stocks and bonds, you generally must pay capital gains taxes for the year in which you sell at a profit. However, with some types of investment property, real estate included, there is a way to defer capital gains taxes, sometimes indefinitely.

It's called the 1031 Exchange. The phrase "like-kind" isn't as limiting as it might seem. It doesn't mean the you must buy a home if you sell a home. Actually, if it's real estate of some kind, it should qualify as a like-kind exchange. Selling land held as an investment and buying a rental home would qualify as a like-kind transaction. The only exception is that you can't use a 1031 Exchange if one property is in the U.S. and the other isn't.

The major limiting factor is that the properties involved must be held for investment. They can't be your personal home or other real estate that isn't a business investment. Ownership of the investment property can be held by an individual, sole proprietor, S Corporation, C Corp, Partnership, or an LLC.

In its simplest form, a 1031 Exchange would involve the simultaneous swap of one property for another. However, this is rarely an available strategy for the investor. The vast majority of 1031 Exchanges are deferred transactions. The first property is sold and the property to be purchased is closed later.

This type of exchange is normally accomplished through a facilitator company or individual called a Qualified Intermediary who brings the two transactions under one umbrella or merged transaction to more resemble a simultaneous swap. The first property is sold and the funds deposited with the facilitator. The property to be purchased is located and the purchase is negotiated. The transaction goes through the same facilitator, keeping the actual investor at arm's-length. The Qualified Intermediary provides the funds from the first sale transaction to close the purchase. Then title is passed to the investor.

The process is highly regulated and has strict time lines. Failure to meet the requirements and time lines will disqualify the transaction and cause the investor to be taxed on the capital gains in that tax year. If it is not a direct swap, as in most cases:

- From the time you sell the first property, you have **45 days** to identify potential replacement properties.
  - o The identification must be in writing and signed by the investor.
  - o It must be delivered to the intermediary (facilitator), not just your real estate agent, accountant or attorney.

- o Replacement properties must be clearly defined, with address and legal description.
- The second time deadline is that the replacement property must be received and the exchange completed no later than **180 days** after the sale of the exchanged property or the due date (with extensions) of the income tax return for the tax year in which the relinquished property was sold, whichever is earlier.
- The replacement property received must be substantially the same as the property identified within the initial 45 day period above.

Title Requirement

One other requirement has stymied some investors in partnerships. The IRS requires that the title to the new property be in the same name/entity as the title to the property that was sold. So, a husband and wife holding an investment property sell it. If a 1031 Exchange is the goal, the new property must be purchased with a title in both their names.

If a corporation sells a property, the new one purchased must be titled to the corporation. The same goes for a partnership. Individual partners can't use funds from the first property's sale to buy another using a 1031 Exchange. They didn't own property, just a share in the partnership.

If a partnership wants to use a 1031 Exchange and some of the partners want to go their own way, the partnership can be liquidated and each partner given a tenant-in-common interest in the property.

Boot

Boot is any item included in a 1031 Exchange that isn't of like-kind. In other words, something other than like-kind real estate changes hands.

There are three common kinds of Boot; Mortgage Boot, Cash Boot and Personal Property Boot.

Mortgage Boot

Mortgage boot is realized in your 1031 Exchange if the property you purchase has a lesser mortgage than the one on the property you sold. If this is the case, you'll be receiving mortgage boot and will be paying capital gains taxes on the difference between the two mortgages. How do you avoid this?

- Make sure the property you're buying has a mortgage equal to or higher than the mortgage on the property you sold.
- Or, add cash to the deal to offset the difference in the two mortgages.

Of course, if the property you're selling has no mortgage, any mortgage at all on the purchased property will satisfy the requirement to avoid mortgage boot.

Cash Boot

By definition, any cash or cash equivalent (example: promissory note) in a 1031 Exchange is not like-kind property and will be considered as Cash Boot and subject to capital gains taxes. If the cash amount is a composite of principal and interest, capital gains taxes will only be charged on the principal amount. However, if you hold the cash and earn interest on it, both the principal and interest will generate a capital gains tax liability.

One trap some investors have run into is having the seller pay for repairs to the property to close the transaction. The dollar value of those repairs will be considered Cash Boot and subject to capital gains taxes.

As you can see, if the property being purchased doesn't have a higher or equal basis or price than the property that was sold, there would have to be some boot somewhere, normally cash boot to go to the investor as the excess left over from the sale and not used in the purchase. So, the investor should be rolling up into a higher priced property or properties.

Personal Property Boot

This is a common situation in rental home 1031 Exchanges, as refrigerators, washers, dryers, or other free-standing appliances or equipment not part of the structure are considered personal property. They aren't real estate for like-kind exchange, and the value of the appliances when they transfer as part of the real estate purchase will be taxed as capital gains.

It's easy to avoid however. In the purchase contract, state specifically that the appliances are NOT included in the sale. Then create a separate bill of sale between the buyer and the seller transferring the appliances for the sum of $1.

Qualified Intermediary or Facilitator Selection

As the investor, you cannot act as your own facilitator. You must choose an independent company or person as your Qualified Intermediary. Keep in mind that this company or individual will be taking your money into their possession from your property sale, so their stability and reputation are critical.

In recent history there are a number of examples of Qualified Intermediaries declaring bankruptcy or having financial difficulties that result in their investor clients losing the funds that were being held on their behalf. Even if the situation can be sorted out and the investor can get their funds, it almost always results in missing the absolute IRS deadlines, and the transaction can no longer be eligible for 1031 Exchange.

An Example

Let's look at an example 1031 Exchange transaction and how it increases equity to reinvest by deferring capital gains taxes. First, to clarify the table, understand that the basis of the property being sold is adjusted by adding the value of capital improvements and subtracting accumulated depreciation. Also, recapture of accumulated depreciation is a capital gains tax item.

Original purchase price of relinquished property	$400,000
Add capital improvements	$40,000
Subtract accumulated depreciation	($60,000)
Adjusted Basis	**$380,000**
Sale price at full market value	$800,000
Less sale expenses	($40,000)
Net Sale Price	$760,000
Realized Gain (Net Sale less the Adjusted Basis)	**$380,000**
Depreciation recapture ($60,000 x 25%)	$15,000
Capital Gains Tax ($380,000 x 15%)	$57,000
Capital Gains Taxes Amount	**$72,000**

Now let's look at the comparison of this as a normal sale and if we use a 1031 Exchange.

	Normal Sale	1031 Exchange
Net Profit (realized gain)	$380,000	$380,000
Total Federal Taxes Due	$72,000	$0
Equity available to reinvest	$308,000	$380,000

This investor was able to roll his profit from the first property into the second and defer capital gains taxes until the second one is ultimately sold … UNLESS

The investor can do the same thing again and again, roll one property into more than one, roll multiple properties into a single one, etc. Capital gains will continue to be deferred indefinitely using the 1031 Exchange process.

Death and Taxes ... or Not?

It can get even better though. If the investor continues this strategy for many years, growing the portfolio from say $400,000 initial purchase until their death.

The property will be valued at fair market value as of the date of death of the investor, and the value will be stepped up. Meaning, if the investor's property as of the date of their death has a fair market value of $2,000,000, the heirs would be allowed to use that stepped up value.

So, they can sell the property right away for the $2,000,000 stepped-up value and owe no capital gains taxes on that amazing growth in value.

You'll never get this kind of break with stocks and bonds. The investor with the same growth in value over time would have had to pay capital gains taxes on the profit in every sale along the way. That's money not available to reinvest.

The 1031 Exchange is one of the greatest tools in building real estate wealth. Take advantage of it.

Chapter 17

Business Structure

BUSINESS:
Sole Propietorship
Partnership
Corporation
Cooperative

From the very beginning, planning and establishing your real estate investing business structure is important. From both liability and tax perspectives, the proper business structure will improve your profitability and reduce your risk. We're going to look at some IRS definitions and categorization of real estate investors, and we'll look at basic business structures like Sole Proprietorship, Corporations and Partnerships. These two broad discussions are related but separate.

A strong advisory is in order here. Spend the time necessary early in your real estate investing business with a qualified accounting professional. Decisions you make and how you form your company can have long-lasting and dramatic tax and liability consequences. Also, since this book is about blue-chip investing, some of these investor categories will not apply if you stick to that business model.

IRS Definitions for Types of Real Estate Investors

"Real Estate Investor" can take on a great many meanings when you're speaking to clients, buyers, sellers and other investors. However, when you're talking to the Internal Revenue Service, there are four main categorizations, and which one the IRS puts you into will make a difference in your tax liability.

1. Real Estate Investor
2. Real Estate Dealer
3. Real Estate Professional
4. Real Estate Developer

The broad definitions of these four categories follow, but they're more complex than can or should be explained here. This will at least give you the basic information you can use in discussions with your accounting professional.

Real Estate Investor

Generally, when just starting out, the investor who has another job or career and owns one or two properties will be considered a real estate investor, passively engaged in investing. This is a person or entity investing in real estate for long term periods (one year or more), in other words, not flipping for profit. You may be able to own a trailer park or campground and still fit into this category. There are limits on how you can treat any paper losses in relation to other income.

Real Estate Dealer

The real estate dealer is someone buying and selling real estate in the short term for profit. If you flip or wholesale, you're likely a dealer. You're a dealer if you buy and sell property fairly quickly, are active in the foreclosure market, or if you buy, rehab and resell properties. You aren't an investor in this case, you're a real estate dealer. You are definitely considered to be operating a real estate business.

Considering you as in the real estate business, the IRS considers the income as active and earned income, not passive. As a real estate dealer, your income is subject to self-employment taxes and will be taxed at normal income tax rates in the year in which you sell the property.

This brings up a tax situation if you sell a property but take back a mortgage on it. While other investor types may be able to take the "installment method" to calculate tax due based on when you actually receive principal payments, a dealer cannot do this. Even if there are payments, the dealer must pay income taxes on the entire amount of the profit in the year realized.

When we talk about LLC or partnership passive business structures later, it's clear that they cannot be used and still qualify as a real estate dealer, as the "passive" nature rules them out. Over time, the courts have applied 15 items used to determine the intent of the investor and whether the property is held primarily for sale or investment:

1. The purpose for acquiring and selling the property
2. The frequency of sales and the number or continuity of sales
3. If the taxpayer uses brokers
4. The ordinary business of the taxpayer
5. Amount of income from property sales related to other sources of income
6. Advertising that's done
7. How long properties are held
8. Activities and time expended by the taxpayer in promoting sales
9. Extent of improvements made to facilitate sales
10. Use of a business office for sales
11. Extent or value of holdings
12. Control over sales representatives
13. Nature and extent of the transactions
14. Any reluctance to sell the property on the part of the seller
15. If the taxpayer desires to liquidate landholdings unexpectedly obtained

Considering all of these, the most important seems to be the number and frequency of sales and the continuity of the business.

Real Estate Developer

A real estate developer is someone who develops property, usually taking raw land, improving it and selling lots, or even homes on land you develop. This is not a great category in which to fall as tax liability goes. A real estate developer may also be engaged in property conversions, such as apartments converting to condominiums.

The tax implications for a developer are significant. All costs that are incurred during the time the property is in development must be capitalized, not deductible in the current year. They can be expensed or amortized later, when the property is put into service or sold, but this could mean a significant tax liability when a property is still held and being developed at the end of the year, a whole lot of expenses will not be deductible, even though paid already.

This can be a major thing, as a project considered a "development" may involve construction or mortgage loan interest, building costs, and other business management costs. These can't be expensed and deducted. It's possible to become an "accidental developer" if you're not careful. This would normally only happen to a residential property rehabber doing extensive work over months. If the use or character of the property is changed, it could be considered a development.

Real Estate Professional

This is a coveted category in which you would like the IRS to place you. It results in significant tax savings. A real estate professional is someone who:

- Owns 5% or more of a real estate business
- Spends a minimum of 750 hours per year working exclusively on real estate activities, OR
- Spends more time on real estate activities than any other income-producing activity, and still meets the minimum 750 hours per year rule.

Tracking your hours well is critical here, as you are in a somewhat higher audit risk category. You don't want to lose the real estate professional status because you can't document the hours you spend in management and business tasks. If you can qualify as a real estate professional, you gain the ability to offset other income with 100% of your real estate losses (real or paper losses). If you can't qualify, you can only offset $25,000 of losses, and only if your adjusted gross income is under $100,000. The $25,000 starts phasing out at $100,000, disappearing completely at $150,000 in income.

The IRS looks at individual properties rather than your activities as a whole. However, proper planning may allow you to group activities and properties to make it easier to meet the 750 hour requirement.

So, What Type of Real Estate Investor Are You?

This can vary based on each transaction, so work with your accounting professional to be certain that you know what you're doing to stick to your business plan. Sticking to the blue-chip real estate investment goal of this book, you should have little difficulty in fitting all of your activities into the proper IRS category and avoiding tax liability surprises. It's still all about working with an accounting person who is thoroughly aware of your business plan and practices.

Business Structure

There are a number of ways in which a business can be structured, and the one you choose can make a significant difference in the amount of your profits you get to keep. However, it's more than just taxes, as liability is also a reason for business structure decisions. Separating your personal assets from the business, and keeping investment risk in the business alone and away from your personal assets is a smart move.

Again, you'll want to be discussing this decision with an accountant and an attorney, as money and liability are their areas of expertise. Just to give you some basics to get the conversations started, let's take a look at the most popular business structures and the characteristics of each. As it's sometimes impossible to switch easily from one type of business structure to another, this decision should be thoroughly investigated up-front so you aren't losing tax or other advantages in a structure switch in a future year.

Sole Proprietorship

This is the simplest and least paperwork-intensive business structure. It's you as an individual, with the business finances inter-mixed with your personal assets. There is no legal distinction between you as the owner and your business. For this reason, any risk or liability you take on in your business will pass through to your personal finances and property. If your rental business is sued by a tenant, your personal assets are at risk as well.

As a sole proprietor, you hold complete ownership in the business and have total control of how it operates and the results. You have no stockholders or partners to consult, and you're completely responsible for the business personally and your personal finances back it up.

Advantages

This is the easiest type of business to start, and you operate as you see fit. You don't have to answer to others, shareholders or partners. You can use the profits any way you like, draw them out or reinvest in the business. You pay income taxes only once at the individual rate. Under certain circumstances, you can write off business losses on your personal taxes. You can dissolve the business as easily as you started it.

Disadvantages

The main disadvantage of the sole proprietorship business structure is the personal liability of the owner. You are personally liable legally for employee issues, debt, and other liabilities. Your personal assets, such as your home, are at risk in the event of a lawsuit. Even a frivolous suit consumes a lot of money in legal fees, and your personal bank accounts and other assets will be involved. Financing is another drawback. For all loans for the business, you're pledging your personal assets as collateral, and many sole proprietorships borrow via personal credit card debt, an expensive way to go.

Legal & Taxes

The sole proprietor can operate under their own name or a trade name, but may need to register the trade name with the state. All legal, zoning, and licensing requirements must be followed as well. You will only pay income tax on your profits at the personal level and once. There are no IRS business taxes.

Partnerships

A Partnership is a legal business structure involving two or more individuals who share the liability, management, and profits. The IRS recognizes several different partnership types, but the two most common are "general" and "limited" partnerships.

The general partnership has two or more owners who share the ownership and management, and they assume liability much as a sole proprietor, just spread among the partners. The limited partnership will have one or more general partners who actually operate the business, and other limited partners who are not involved in the operation and management, only participating as investors. This can also be called a LLP, or Limited Liability Partnership.

When a partnership is formed, a Partnership Agreement document is created. This document is important, as it sets out how the partnership will operate, how decisions are to be made and by whom, and how disputes are to be resolved.

Advantages

The major advantage of a partnership is the tax treatment it enjoys. The business or partnership entity is not taxed. Tax liability is incurred when income and profits are passed through to the individual partners. Each partner files the appropriate tax forms and is liable for their individual taxes on the income received from the partnership.

Of course, another advantage is the ability to pool the resources of the partners to fund the startup and operations of the company. A partnership also can pool the knowledge and experience of the partners to complement each other and create a stronger company with greater potential.

Disadvantages

Personal liability is a major concern, as in a general partnership each partner is liable for decisions, actions and obligations of the partnership. This is where a clear Partnership Agreement is necessary to clearly set out what each partner can do and how they can or cannot obligate the partnership in contracts or debts.

The limited partnership (or LLP) can shield some partners from liability, but it's a more complex business organization, with complex administration and required forms and filings.

Legal & Taxes

A major portion of the Partnership Agreement will be a thorough treatment of how the partnership can be bound and by whom. How will the ownership be shared and in what ratios? There must be a very clear description of how decisions will be made, and how disputes will be resolved.

There will also be detailed processes for deciding how and when to distribute profits to partners. Another key portion of the Partnership Agreement will be the section that describes how a partner leaving will be compensated and how their ownership interest will be handled.

As previously mentioned, the partnership isn't taxed as a separate entity. Tax liability passes to the individual partners when income is withdrawn.

Corporations

A corporation is an entity created at state level, and it's a separate legal entity from its members or shareholders. This legal entity has privileges and liabilities that are only its own, not transferred to the members or shareholders. There are several different popular forms of corporation, most of which are formed to conduct business and take advantage of specific privileges and tax treatments only available to the corporate entity.

Advantages

One of the main advantages of the corporate structure is limited liability. If a corporation has financial difficulties or fails, shareholders may lose their individual investments, but they will not be liable for the debts of the corporation. There are four characteristics of the business corporation:

- Legal personality
- Limited liability
- Transferable ownership shares
- Centralized management with a board of directors

Though it's a business entity and not a person, corporations are recognized by law to have certain rights and responsibilities just as individuals do. A corporation can break the law, and be taken to court for violations or damages. When created, corporations are considered eternal or immortal entities, but they can be "dissolved." This dissolution can be voluntary by the shareholders, or it can be forced by a court or other statutory operation.

Corporate statutes empower corporations to not only do business, but to own property, sign binding contracts, and to pay taxes as a separate entity from the shareholder owners. As the corporate form shields individual shareholders from liability for actions and debts of the corporation, it also shields the corporation from claims against individual shareholders. Creditors of the corporation do hold priority over shareholders in liquidations.

Disadvantages

One disadvantage of the corporate form of business structure is the separate identity for taxation. Taxes are in effect paid twice on profits. The corporation is taxed at the corporate level, and when dividends are paid to pass profits to the shareholders, they're taxed again at the individual shareholder level. Some shareholders consider it a disadvantage to have only a vote when they perceive that the board of directors or management aren't doing a good job of running the company.

Legal & Taxes

Taxes have already been mentioned under disadvantages. The government gets to double-dip when the profits are taxed at corporate level and again when distributed to shareholders. Legally, the corporation shields shareholders from liability, and the corporation itself can be found in violation of laws as a separate entity. That's not to say that members of the board or upper management can't be charged with crimes if they violate laws. There are many prior top-level corporate managers in prisons today for violations of trading, business, or other laws.

C and S Corporations

When a corporation is formed, the IRS considers it as having been formed as a "C" Corporation. This is one that is taxed separately from its shareholders. However, then the money distributed to shareholders is taxed again at the individual level. This is the predominate corporate formation.

If an S Corporation is elected when the company is formed, then the disadvantage of double taxation is avoided. There are some rules as to who can elect S Corporation status. An S Corporation passes tax liability through to the shareholders, much as we discussed in the Partnership structure.

The LLC, Limited Liability Company

The IRS does a good job of explaining the LLC on their site here: http://www.irs.gov/businesses/small/article/0,,id=98277,00.html   Here is what they say:

A Limited Liability Company (LLC) is a business structure allowed by state statute. LLCs are popular because, similar to a corporation, owners have limited personal liability for the debts and actions of the LLC. Other features of LLCs are more like a partnership, providing management flexibility and the benefit of pass-through taxation.

Owners of an LLC are called members. Since most states do not restrict ownership, members may include individuals, corporations, other LLCs and foreign entities. There is no maximum number of members. Most states also permit "single member" LLCs, those having only one owner.

A few types of businesses generally cannot be LLCs, such as banks and insurance companies. Check your state's requirements and the federal tax regulations for further information. There are special rules for foreign LLCs.

Classifications

The federal government does not recognize an LLC as a classification for federal tax purposes. An LLC business entity must file a corporation, partnership or sole proprietorship tax return.

An LLC that is not automatically classified as a corporation can file Form 8832 to elect their business entity classification. A business with at least 2 members can choose to be classified as an association taxable as a corporation or a partnership, and a business entity with a single member can choose to be classified as either an association taxable as a corporation or disregarded as an entity separate from its owner, a "disregarded entity." Form 8832 is also filed to change the LLC's classification.

LLCs have become popular due to the ability to structure for limited liability like a corporation, but to also elect not to be taxed as a corporation.

Can One Person Form an LLC?

As the LLC is a popular company structure for real estate investment, this is a common question. In most states it is possible for a single person to form an LLC for a real estate investment business. Check with your accountant about your state's law.

When you do form an LLC, you'll have several documents, and we'll go through some sample information and the documents to give you an idea of what should be considered. These are from one state, but there will be similarities across states in the forms and considerations.

Certificate of Formation

This document is filed at the state and declares the formation of the Limited Liability Company. It states the name under which the company will operate, as well as:

- the minimum number of members
- when and how the LLC can be terminated or dissolved
- a description of the business to be conducted, in this case real estate investment

It is signed by the Managers/Members and notarized.

Articles of Organization

In this document, the members or organizers of the LLC certify the LLC name, county where located, and addresses, as well as dissolution timing again. This will vary by state, as there is frequently a requirement to clearly identify the life of the company and when/how it can be dissolved.

This document may describe the status of the owners and define them, as Managers, Members, or both. There is also another statement of the purpose of the business and any limitations on the authority of Members and/or Managers.

Operating Agreement

This is a long document and may appear daunting, but it's really fairly simple, describing the rules under which the LLC members will operate. It's the relationship agreement that sets out who does what, who has certain authority and who doesn't, liabilities, management roles and how and when profits will be passed to members.

Witness of Intent

The document begins with the statement that those signing are agreeing to form the business for the stated purpose of real estate investment.

Organization

Here the LLC is named and the state where it is being formed. If operating under other names as well, they'll be mentioned here. The duration of operation will be stated and referred back to the Articles of Organization.

This area provides names and addresses of Managers and the Registered Office location and Resident Agent for the LLC. This area may specifically state that this is not a partnership, but that partnership tax treatment is desired.

Books, Records and Accounting

This section states that the books and records will be maintained and housed at the Registered Office, and that they will comply with state laws and LLC operation rules.

There will also be a statement of the accounting or fiscal year for accounting purposes. This area may also designate the company's accountant or accounting firm if that's where records will be held.

This section will describe reports to be maintained and their frequency. There will also be specific statements as to separate capital accounting for members to adequately account for capital contributions of the members. This will account for not only money, but property that's contributed to the business by Members.

Basically, this is an accounting function to track what is invested and what is withdrawn by each Member. So, when distributions are made, they are reflected here. The rules here will be stated to be as required by the appropriate state code.

Capital Contributions

In the formation of the LLC, Members will be contributing money or other property to set up the company for operations. In this section the rules for these contributions will be set out, and may outline specific amounts by Member here, but more likely in an attached Exhibit.

This section discusses if there will be future or ongoing requirements for investment and capital contributions, and what action can be taken if a member fails to make a required capital contribution.

Allocations and Distributions

Here is where the plan for when and distributions will be and how they will be determined. Generally, here is where the statement is made that distributions, whenever calculated, will be distributed based on the ratio of ownership of the Members. There may also be a statement that distributions are not allowed to the extent they may jeopardize the ability of the LLC to pay the bills.

Distribution of Membership Interests

In this section, the ways in which Members' ownership interest can be disposed of is laid out in detail. The reasons why a Member could be leaving the LLC, permitted ways they can leave, if they can assign or convey their rights in any way, and other details as to distribution of their ownership will be detailed.

Meetings & Voting

Frequency of meetings and rules for voting by members will be detailed here. This area will also discuss voting to dissolve the LLC, and how other items to be voted upon can be submitted by Members.

Management

Managers and how they will be appointed or elected will be in this section. Any compensation of managers will be discussed here as well. Manager duties will be described in detail here.

The powers of managers and the restrictions on their powers will be defined here. Who can bind the company to contracts or borrow on behalf of the LLC will be laid out in this area.

Liability & Indemnification

The all-important exculpation of liability on the part of Members and Managers for actions of the LLC is laid out here. Remember that this is one of the reasons for using an LLC structure, as liability can be minimized while enjoying partnership-like tax advantages.

Miscellaneous & More Dissolution Items

A host of details not previously covered in other sections will be dealt with here. Things like notices, binding effect, governing laws and severability can be in this section.

Exhibits

As mentioned earlier, there will probably be an exhibit here detailing the capital contributions of each Member. There can be other exhibits that cover items or lists of a specific nature. If real estate or other property is contributed, there could be details and even legal descriptions and deeds in an exhibit.

Now you will have the basic business structure knowledge to have productive discussions with your attorney and accountant and to make the appropriate decision for the formation of your new business.

Chapter 18

Where are the Blue-chip homes?

A question that comes up frequently at real estate seminars and classes is about the application of the process "where they live." Everyone's familiar with the fact that real estate really is a localized market. While the prices in any particular area will respond to national and regional market conditions, ultimately the local economy, employment and population demographics will be the primary influences on real estate prices and rentals.

However, while some areas have stronger rental markets than others or may be tougher areas in which to locate blue-chip properties, the concepts and strategies you've been exposed to in this book will work where you live. Let's jump around the country a bit and use online resources to uncover investment opportunities.

Since we're jumping around online, but not flying or driving, we're not going to know the areas in detail or be able to do the full due diligence to make sure these are truly blue-chip properties and neighborhoods. However, we'll try to use properties that fit as many of our criteria as possible.

The goal of this exercise is to show you that there is enough opportunity out there in so many diverse parts of the country that you can find a blue-chip rental property that will meet your investment objectives. We'll not go into detail with all of the profit metrics discussed in previous chapters, but will do enough math for each example to show that it will be a great investment if all of our blue-chip criteria are met.

Here's how we'll do this exercise. We're going to use Realtor.com to locate homes for sale, and Rent.com to find current rental properties to get an example rent income. We'll take one for-sale home and one rental home in the same zip code or within 5 miles of each other, and with the same bedroom/bath configuration and other characteristics. We're not going to get into buying at a lower price, which we would normally be able to do. And, we'll use the built-in mortgage payment estimate at Realtor.com.

All of the homes will be less than 20 years old, most newer, as we're looking for descriptions that speak to being in great-to-excellent condition and ready to move in. They will also fit our median price goals to fit the needs of a majority of area renters. Let's travel.

Houston, TX

Zip Code: 77047

Basic home configuration: 3 BR, 2 BA, 2 car garage

List selling price for home: $83,000

Description: This beautiful LENNAR family home has a Stone elevation, Berber carpet, alarm system, & no back neighbors. Huge Master suite with walk-in closet, garden tub, separate shower and dual vanities. Kitchen has 42" cabinets, tile floors, open to family room and dining for great family entertainment. It has a Leaded front door & powder room has great added storage space. The home is minutes from the Medical Center, 288, Beltway 8 .

Rental home advertised rent: $1195

Description: "Charming home built in 2010 and only lived in for 6 months. 2 minutes to 288, 15 minutes to downtown and 10 minutes to Med Center."

Approx. cash flow/month, taxes/insurance included: $650

Charlotte, NC

Zip Code: 28215

Basic home configuration: 3 BR, 3 BA, 2 car garage

List selling price for home: $84,900

Description:

- County: Mecklenburg
- Area: 02 - Mecklenburg County (E)
- Approximately 0.12 acre(s)
- 2 total full baths
- 1 total half bath
- 2 stories
- Kitchen
- 1 car garage
- Cooling features: Central Air
- Inclusions: Dishwasher, Disposal, Security System
- Community features: Playground, Pond, Walking Trails
- Corner lot
- Lot size is less than 1/2 acre
- Utilities present: City Sewer, City Water
- Call agent for details on association fee info.
- Dining room
- Laundry room
- Main Floor Bathroom
- Master Bedroom

Rental home advertised rent: $1200

Description:

- Air conditioning
- Cable/Satellite Ready
- Carpeting
- Ceiling Fan
- Central Heat and Air
- Crown Molding
- Gas Fireplace
- Hardwood Floors
- Walk-In Closets

Approx. cash flow/month, taxes/insurance included: $650

Indianapolis, IN

Zip Code: 46168

Basic home configuration: 3 BR, 2 BA

List selling price for home: $108,000

Description:

- Approximately 0.15 acre(s)
- 2 total full bath(s)
- 5 total rooms
- Kitchen
- Living room is 15x17,Carpeting,Main Level,Window Treatments
- Kitchen is 12x14, Vinyl Floor, Main Level, Window Treatments
- Laundry room is 6x6, Vinyl Floor, Main Level
- 2 car garage(s)

- Attached parking
- Forced air heat
- Cooling features: Central Electric,Cooling
- Community park(s)
- Approximate lot is 65x106
- Lot features: Sidewalks, Small Trees, Storm Sewer, Street Lights
- Lot size is less than 1/2 acre
- Utilities present: Municipal Sewer, Municipal Water, Cable Connection, Gas Available, High Speed Internet Available
- Call agent for details on association fee info.
- School District: Plainfield Community
- Laundry room
- Main Floor Bedroom
- Main Floor Bathroom
- Living Room
- Master Bedroom
- Parking features: Garage Door Opener

Rental home advertised rent: $1200

Description: "3BR 2.5BA HOUSE FOR RENT. 2 CAR GARAGE. GREAT SCHOOLS. CLOSE TO I-70."

Approx. cash flow/month, taxes/insurance included: $480

Punta Gorda, FL

Zip Code: 33955

Basic home configuration: 3 BR, 3 BA, 2 car garage

List selling price for home: $99,900

Description:

- Subdivision: Punta Gorda Isles Sec 16
- Approximately 0.23 acre(s)
- 2 total full bath(s)
- Kitchen
- Master Bedroom is 12x14
- Living room is 12x10
- Kitchen is 12x10
- 2 car garage(s)
- Attached parking
- Cooling features: Central
- Lot size is less than 1/2 acre
- Topography: Conservation Area
- Utilities present: Public Utilities
- Living Room
- Master Bedroom
- Parking features: 2 Car Garage

Rental home advertised rent: $1200

Description: "Well maintained, 5 years old, great location, easy access to both Rt. 41 and Rt. 75"

Approx. cash flow/month, taxes/insurance included: $575

Colorado Springs, CO

Zip Code: 80922

Basic home configuration: 3 BR, 2 BA, 2 story, 2 car garage

List selling price for home: $125,000

Description:

- Approximately 0.08 acre(s)
- 2 stories
- Type: Single Family, Wood Frame
- Basement is 378 Basement SqFt
- 2 car garage(s)
- Attached parking
- Forced air heat
- Cooling features: Ceiling Fan
- Lot features: Level
- Located on a cul-de-sac
- Lot size is less than 1/2 acre
- Development status: Existing Home
- School District: 49-Falcon
- Basement
- Parking features: Garage Door Opener

Rental home advertised rent: $1295

Description: Former Richmond Model Home - Sparkling Clean and situated on a cul-de-sac in popular Springs Ranch - Central Air, Whole House Humidifier, Beautifully landscaped, Intercom

Approx. cash flow/month, taxes/insurance included: $460

Jackson, MS

Zip Code: 39206

Basic home configuration: 4 BR, 2 BA, garage

List selling price for home: $114,900

Description:

- 1 stories
- 1 car garage

- Cooling features: Ceiling Fan(s),Cooling
- Inclusions: Cooktop, Dishwasher, Disposal, Dryer, Refrigerator, Vent Hood, Wall Oven (Single), Washer, Garage Door Opener, Satellite Dish, Smoke Detectors, Water Heater
- Utilities present: Sewer Connected, Public Water
- Elementary School: North Jackson
- Middle School: Powell
- High School: Callaway
- Laundry room

Rental home advertised rent: $1600

Description: This is a very spacious house on 1+ acres of land. It has carpeted throughout, two car garage and fenced in back yard. Central heating and air and a large laundry room!

Approx. cash flow/month, taxes/insurance included: $680

It will work where you live.

These were very quick evaluations on the Web, but there were many choices. Actually one of the more difficult jobs was to find rentals in some areas. Fewer rentals in the neighborhood is one of our desired blue-chip criteria.

Chapter 19

Now Is the Time to Secure Your Future

A major stumbling hurdle to successful blue-chip real estate investing has been removed for you. You have the knowledge in this book, and it's everything you need for rental property investment in blue-chip properties.

Knowing how to do something doesn't always produce results however. People are hesitant to put new knowledge into practice, especially when it involves large dollar amounts or a mortgage.

However, if not now, when? Remember our discussion of the perfect storm in rental property investment back in Chapter 8.

Home prices began an extended downturn in 2007, and nationally the average by 2010 was more than 30% below the price highs around 2006. In the hardest-hit areas, price reductions of more than 50% were common.

OK, but that doesn't mean they'll be that way forever. No, eventually reasonable price appreciation will return. However, it takes eager buyers for that to happen, and those are rare and expected to remain at a low level for years.

There is plenty of support for the theory that the U.S. is going to be a nation of renters for many years into the future. Home ownership rates aren't poised for a comeback anytime soon. So, there's going to be a continued increase in demand for quality rental homes.

Along with few buyers, lower prices and more renters, interest rates took a dive and are expected to remain below 30 year averages for a long time. It costs far less to buy and finance a property, and you can charge above-market rents for blue-chip properties. This means that cash flow and overall return on your investment will be higher than at most points in history.

Though this window of opportunity is expected to last for years, why pass up years of positive cash flow and even some appreciation. The sooner the better seems the best approach as far as investments go. Stocks and bonds are OK, but every investor should be diversifying into real estate.

So, you want to get to it, what's next? Where you are in your investments and financial abilities will determine where you jump into this series of steps, but you want to get moving by getting to the specifics. Take a ten-step approach.

1. Assess your current financial situation and your current investments.

2. Determine where you have investable funds or assets to get into your first rental property.
3. Talk to an accountant and attorney, or several if you need to select, and make sure your plan is sound.
4. If you have retirement accounts, can one or more be converted to a self-directed IRA or other account in which you can do rental property investment.
5. Start researching your local market, and work with a Realtor or real estate investment company to get automated listing reports.
6. Read the math and leverage chapters again and practice some of the valuation math.
7. Begin to identify possible blue-chip properties, and apply our blue-chip selection criteria to narrow down your list.
8. Compare your investment objectives, your financial ability to purchase and your properties short-list.
9. Do more area, market, and neighborhood research, including the strength of the rental market and the expected return on investment from each of your short-list properties.
10. Select a property and make an offer!

Sure, there are interim steps or items involved in each of these ten steps, but this is the approach you should take to get started. You'll only be taking that rent check to the bank by taking action to secure your future.

Appendix

Introduction to Investor Nation

We've covered a lot of ground in this book, and you have the tools and resources to move forward with a blue-chip real estate investment business plan. The authors, owners and operators of Investor Nation, want you to know that you're ready to create and manage a successful real estate rental property management business with what you've learned here.

However, we also discussed companies that bring together service packages for investors, some including the properties themselves, and the problems that can destroy profits if the company isn't experienced and properly staffed. We provided that information because we wanted you to know how to evaluate a company. Here is more about Investor Nation, and we're here for help and consultation.

Who We Are

The authors of this book own and operate Investor Nation, and years of experience in the rental real estate business, both as investors and as a provider of services to investors, brought about our desire to publish this guide.

The company was formed in 2009 in response to the real estate crisis in high gear at that time, and continuing to indicate real problems for homeowners and borrowers in this country. There is always opportunity in every situation, even one as dire as the housing and mortgage market crash.

We formed the company with the purpose of examining the various residential real estate asset types and identifying those with the highest potential for stable yields and future growth ... blue-chip investments. Since 2009, Investor Nation has honed the Blue-Chip Real Estate Investment philosophy, not only building out a tested and successful strategy, but also a team for successful implementation.

Our team of property managers, contractors, closing attorneys, CPAs and others have assisted people from around the U.S. and the world to purchase and manage high quality single family homes and enjoy the rewards of blue-chip real estate investment.

Our Services

As illustrated by the resources and information we've delivered in this book, Investor Nation brings all of these strategies, techniques, evaluation, negotiation and management functions together into a client service package for real estate investment success.

Real Estate Opportunities

A gateway is provided by Investor Nation at http://investornation.com for clients to locate secure blue-chip real estate investment opportunities. At the time of this writing, the company offers real estate rental investment opportunities in Tennessee, New York, and Florida.

Client Advisory

As you moved through the chapters of this book, you learned about a great many functions and facets of rental real estate investment, and Investor Nation provides an integrated approach to advising clients in their proper implementation for profits:

- market analysis
- property sourcing
- due diligence
- financing
- insurance
- closing
- property management

Using the knowledge gained in this book, clients then take advantage of our extended team of experts to execute the processes with total confidence.

Proprietary Services

Due to process complexity and a desire to give Investor Nation clients a strategic advantage, we have developed proprietary models for property sourcing and evaluation. We apply these models to the universe of available properties to drill down to those that have conformed to both quantitative and qualitative standards we've developed.

One of the proprietary products developed by the authors and Investor Nation owners is RealYields, a property analysis application. More information on this unique application is available at http://realyields.com.

Investor Intelligence

Once the cash is flowing from rental property investments, there can't be a relaxation of ongoing due diligence. The market is changing as you're reading this. Not all changes are going to have an influence on our clients' investments, but it's our job to provide ongoing market intelligence and advice to keep clients informed about trends and actions that may need to be taken to avoid problems or to take advantage of situations for profit.

At http://investornation.com/intelligence, investors can view housing market data and news relevant to rental real estate investing. This isn't just a rehash of information from publications and the Internet, as much of it has been developed directly by Investor Nation analysts and investment banks with which Investor Nation has relationships.

If you're not yet a client, there is complimentary information at the above URL, and our clients have protected access to much more extensive market intelligence.

About the Authors

Stephen Green

President, Co-Founder

Stephen joined as President of Investor Nation in January 2009 to manage the company's daily operations including property sourcing/acquisition, due diligence and bank financing. He is also a key manager of contractor, property management, and fund raising relationships.

Stephen earned his bachelor's degree in Marketing from Auburn University in May 2005. After graduation he held sales and project management roles in the housing and financial sector. From May to December 2005 he was an Account Manager for Jeld-Wen Windows and Doors and then was an Account Representative for Fidelity Investments until July 2006.

Prior to becoming part of the Investor Nation team, Stephen managed his own contracting company to assist out-of-state investors with the renovation and financing of single-family homes. He has partnered with Co-Founder Ryan Hinricher on over 500 real estate transactions since 2007. Stephen is a Memphis native and was awarded the rank of Eagle Scout in 2000.

Ryan Hinricher

Portfolio Manager, Founder

Ryan Hinricher is a professional real estate investor, housing market analyst, and change advocate. He is the founder of Investor Nation, a value-added real estate opportunity firm. Hinricher spent 10 years in the banking business as an analyst, underwriter, and branch manager. He's owned investment property since 2000.

Hinricher is a founder and member of the Executive Committee of RealYields, an industry-leading property analysis and feasibility application.

Hinricher is a member of the American Real Estate and Urban Economics Association and the Urban Land Institute. He has been active in the community with Habitat-for-Humanity.

Hinricher is a former housing market columnist for Bigger Pockets and has been quoted by the Wall Street Journal, The Real Deal, The Scotsman Guide, Classified Intelligence, Minyanville, WallStreet 24/7, Realtor Magazine, Realty 411, Personal Real Estate Investor, HSH.com, US Chamber of Commerce, and the book, The Complete Guide to Locating and Profiting from Emerging Real Estate Markets.

Appendix II

Frequently Asked Questions

We've covered the process thoroughly in this guide to blue-chip real estate investing, but there are a few questions we hear from clients and others. Let's get those answered for you here.

Exactly what services do you provide?

We're a turnkey rental real estate investment services provider in the Memphis, TN market. This includes portfolio consultation, exit strategy development, due diligence, acquisition, financing, inspection, closing, insurance and property management. All the functions for success are covered.

What types of neighborhoods are your focus?

You can get more detail in our property and neighborhood evaluation chapters, however our neighborhood criteria include:

- Close proximity to major employers.
- Close proximity to big-box retailers.
- Projected to experience population growth.
- Average or below average crime.
- Prices near the market median home price range.
- Primarily owner-occupied.

These have proven to be the most effective evaluation criteria to assure profits and appreciation.

Is there a typical home price range?

Investor Nation investment homes tend to fall into a range between $75,000 and $150,000.

Does Investor Nation make financing available?

We work on our clients' behalf with banks and mortgage lenders both locally and around the country. We also, when it's good for the investment, offer an owner-financing model.

Can real estate agents be involved and earn a commission?

We work with real estate professionals, especially those who are experienced and deliver properties that meet our stringent evaluation criteria.

How does the purchase and closing process work?

Once the investor identifies a property, Investor Nation provides a state realty board approved contract. If financing is required, we handle adding the appropriate contingencies, and the closing usually takes place within 30 days. If a cash deal, closing can happen within 7 to 10 days from contract. Rents are prorated, so the new owner receives any due from closing.

Can I inspect the home before the deal is final?

You certainly can. We allow a 7-day "cold feet" policy on all contracts. During that period, have any inspections done that you desire, and we'll help to facilitate the process using inspectors of your choice. We'll provide a copy of any inspections we've completed as well.

What if there's a problem after I purchase?

Investor Nation enjoys a great reputation and considerable repeat business. After all, success in rental property investment brings a desire to add to holdings, and we want to be your resource. So, you can always call Investor Nation and we will help you to troubleshoot any issue you might have with the property.

How do you screen tenants?

Investor Nation knows that reliable tenants and on-time rents are the foundation of a great investment. We do both credit and criminal background checks on every prospective tenant. We also verify income sufficient to cover their rent and other obligations.

How is property maintenance handled?

The property manager receives all property maintenance and repair calls, handling pre-agreed minor maintenance for you. Major repairs will not be done until consulting with you as the owner. There is no markup of maintenance and repair costs; they are billed to the owner at cost.

We hope you're up to speed now, but we're here to answer any other questions you may have with a goal of creating highly successful rental real estate investors.